From Vulnerability to

From Vulnerability to Resilience
A framework for analysis and action to build community resilience

Katherine Pasteur

PRACTICAL ACTION
Publishing

Practical Action Publishing Ltd
Schumacher Centre for Technology and Development
Bourton on Dunsmore, Rugby,
Warwickshire CV23 9QZ, UK
www.practicalactionpublishing.org

ISBN 978 1 85339 718 9

Since 1974, Practical Action Publishing (formerly Intermediate Technology Publications and ITDG Publishing) has published and disseminated books and information in support of international development work throughout the world. Practical Action Publishing is a trading name of Practical Action Publishing Ltd (Company Reg. No. 1159018), the wholly owned publishing company of Practical Action. Practical Action Publishing trades only in support of its parent charity objectives and any profits are covenanted back to Practical Action (Charity Reg. No. 247257, Group VAT Registration No. 880 9924 76).

Cover photos: A woman in Bangladesh pumps water on a plinth raised above flood level; and farmers in Nepal repair irrigation channels damaged by a river. Credit: Practical Action
Cover design by Practical Action Publishing
Typeset by S.J.I. Services, New Delhi
Printed by Hobbs the Printers Ltd

CONTENTS

FIGURES

TABLES

PREFACE

From vulnerability to resilience: What is the V2R framework?

From vulnerability to resilience, or V2R, is a framework for analysis and action to reduce vulnerability and strengthen the resilience of individuals, households and communities. The framework sets out the key factors that contribute to peoples' vulnerability: exposure to hazards and stresses; fragile livelihoods; future uncertainty; and weak governance. It provides detailed explanations of the linkages between these factors, as well as ideas for action to strengthen resilience.

The framework was developed to address the need to work in a more integrated way and to tackle the causes and consequences of vulnerability. It was initially developed under the project, Mainstreaming Livelihood-centred Approaches to Disaster Management (funded by the Department for International Development's Conflict and Humanitarian Fund 2006–2010), which aimed to integrate analysis and action around strengthening livelihoods and disaster preparedness for reducing disaster risk. However, it became increasingly urgent to incorporate a more dynamic analysis of the long term trends which contribute to growing uncertainty for poor people about the future, not least amongst these being climate change. The V2R framework fully integrates climate analysis and action within an existing holistic approach which can be applied in many situations.

Audience for the V2R

The V2R framework has been written with the needs and interests of Practical Action programme staff in mind. However, the issues and principles in the document are also relevant to a much wider audience including practitioners (NGOS and local government staff), researchers, and policymakers working in livelihoods, disaster management and climate change adaptation. It is intended to provide guidance to the reader, rather than dictate a set way of doing things. The material can also be adapted to suit communication to other audiences such as community-based organizations (CBOs).

Structure of the document

This document is organized into four parts.

Part One provides a general introduction to the rationale behind developing an integrated framework and outlines the key concepts underlying the V2R approach.

Part Two systematically describes the different elements of the framework: vulnerability and resilience; hazards and stresses; livelihoods; future uncertainty; and governance. It highlights the linkages between the different elements and provides examples of action drawing on Practical Action's own experience.

Part Three suggests practical steps in carrying out an analysis of vulnerability and resilience, providing checklists of questions and example tools. It also describes a number of different ways in which the framework and analysis can be used to guide action – for planning, for adapting, or for monitoring and evaluating projects or programmes and for carrying out training.

Part Four consists of a selection of reference materials which support and supplement the information contained in the earlier parts of this document. They provide more detail on particular approaches, models and tools which complement the V2R framework.

Throughout the document, Case Studies are used to illustrate different elements of the framework and Issues Pages explore cross-cutting themes such as gender, technology and climate change.

ACKNOWLEDGEMENTS

The V2R framework and this publication are the result of much collaborative thinking and practice amongst the Reducing Vulnerability Team in the UK and internationally. I would like to give huge thanks to everyone both within Practical Action and beyond who contributed to their production, through sharing ideas, field testing, suggesting case studies, and providing useful comments and feedback at various stages: they are far too many to name. Special mention must go, however, to Piet van den Ende and Hilary Warburton for their support and guidance throughout this lengthy process.

I would like to acknowledge the Conflict, Humanitarian And Security Department (CHASE) at the Department for International Development (DFID) for their financial support to the project Mainstreaming a Livelihoods Centred Approach to Disaster Risk Reduction, under which this publication was produced.

ACRONYMS

AGRITEX	Agricultural Extension Services
CAP	Community Action Planning
CBO	Community-Based Organization
CBP	Community-Based Planning
DDR	Donor-Driven Reconstruction
DDRM	Decentralized Disaster Risk Management
DFID	Department for International Development, UK
DRR	Disaster Risk Reduction
EC	European Commission
FAO	Food and Agriculture Organization of the United Nations
FEWSNET	Famine Early Warning Systems Network
FIVIMS	Food Insecurity and Vulnerability Information and Mapping
GMO	Genetically Modified Organisms
IPCC	Intergovernmental Panel on Climate Change
IPR	Intellectual Property Rights
M&E	Monitoring and Evaluation
MDG	Millennium Development Goals
NGO	Non-Government Organization
OCHA	Office for the Coordination of Humanitarian Affairs
PAR	Pressure and Release
PCR	People-Centred Reconstruction
PTD	Participatory Technology Development
UK	United Kingdom
UN	United Nations
UNEP	United Nations Environmental Programme
UNESCO	United Nations Educational, Scientific and Cultural Organization
UNISDR	United Nations International Strategy for Disaster Reduction
UNOSAT	United Nations Operational Satellite Applications Programme
V2R	Vulnerability to Resilience
VDC	Village Development Committee
WDC	Women's Development Committee
WMO	World Meteorological Organization

PART 1
INTRODUCTION

1.1 FROM VULNERABILITY TO RESILIENCE

From Vulnerability to Resilience (V2R) is an approach and framework (see Figure 1 below) that brings together several core areas for development programming to move people permanently out of poverty, namely strengthening livelihoods, disaster preparedness, building adaptive capacity and addressing different areas of the governance environment. The goal is to address the multidimensional nature of poverty through an integrated approach that considers all of the core factors underlying vulnerability.

The context for a multidimensional approach

Three out of four poor people in developing countries live in rural areas (UNDP, 2007). Of these, most live in fragile environments such as arid or mountainous areas often at long distances from markets and other services. They have few resources at their disposal and have inadequate access to skills and technologies that could help them to make best use of those resources. Therefore their income earning options are limited and their ability to diversify or adapt when circumstances change is constrained. Poor people also often live in risk-prone areas such as on steep slopes, river embankments or floodplains because they cannot afford to live in safer areas. The impacts of drought and floods are often exacerbated by unsustainable development such as deforestation or a combination of increasing population pressure, political tensions and economic changes that lead to practices that cause environmental degradation. Conflict is fuelled by easy access to weapons and the increasing competition over scarce resources such as pasture and water.

In the event of hazards, the poor and their livelihoods tend to be the hardest hit. The livelihoods of marginal and small farmers, artisans and fishermen are affected through the loss of assets, loss of food sources (crops or stores) and loss of employment or income earning opportunities. When disaster strikes they may be forced to take desperate measures to survive such as abandoning their homes or selling vital land or tools on which their livelihoods depend because they have no savings or other alternatives. This undermines their future recovery and each shock can drive them deeper into poverty. The poor are often politically marginalized and have little voice in the policy or institutional decisions that affect them. Services, such as schooling, health, extension, transport and markets are often inadequate or unavailable to people living in more remote or challenging areas. They lack the safety nets that are taken for granted in richer countries, such as savings, insurance policies or government services to warn and protect them from disasters.

Growing uncertainty is a further characteristic of the lives of the poorest. As the world becomes more interconnected, the livelihoods of the poor can be affected by events happening in distant parts of the world. Financial markets can affect prices for staple crops in developing countries.

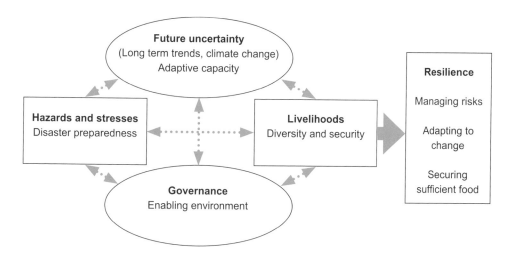

Figure 1. Resilience framework

Policy shifts, for example towards biofuels, can contribute to rising grain prices and urban food shortages. The impact of climate change is being felt directly by increasing numbers of people as changing seasons and more extreme weather patterns affect the natural environment that people depend on and contribute to crop failures and livestock losses, thus tipping the balance between survival and destitution. Poverty, vulnerability and disasters are closely related and cannot be viewed in isolation from one another. These multiple factors: lack of resources; fragile livelihoods; exposure to hazards; climate change and other trends; and weak institutional support mechanisms must be understood in a more integrated manner in order to seek effective ways to address them.

Benefits of integration

There are strong arguments in favour of integrating these approaches under one framework for analysis and action. Disasters can significantly compromise development progress, reduce the effectiveness of aid investments and halt or slow progress towards achieving the Millennium Development Goals (MDGs). Relevant actions to reduce disaster risk can save lives and prevent huge economic losses. Furthermore, aid resources which are diverted to humanitarian and emergency responses can reduce the aid available for development programmes elsewhere in areas not directly affected by disasters. It has been estimated that every US$1 spent on disaster reduction saves $3 in terms of the reduced impact of disasters (Benn, 2006) In Vietnam, replanting coastal mangroves at relatively low cost resulted in dramatic reductions in lives lost and crops destroyed during typhoons. There have also been knock-on benefits on livelihoods as the mangroves provide an opportunity for sustainable harvesting of sea products such as baby crab (IFRC, 2002).

1.2 LINKS WITH OTHER APPROACHES

Until relatively recently, the disasters, longer term development (for sustainable livelihoods) and climate change communities tended to operate in parallel, often working in different departments within organizations or under different government agencies and using different frameworks or approaches to shape their work. Practical Action's V2R Framework draws on these existing frameworks and approaches relating to sustainable livelihoods, disaster management and climate change adaptation, aiming to combine the key elements into one integrated model. Practitioners can refer back to these models, further details of which are provided in **Section 4.1**.

Sustainable livelihoods

The sustainable livelihoods approach is a holistic, people-centred approach to understanding and addressing the multiple factors that influence poverty and well-being. This approach has been used by a number of agencies, most notably the UK Department for International Development (DFID) which produced a detailed framework and guidance materials (see **Section 4.1.1**).

The V2R draws heavily on sustainable livelihoods thinking in recognizing the importance of having access to a diverse range of assets or resources, including social influence and voice, and sustainable technologies, in order to provide vulnerable people with safer livelihood options and coping strategies in times of need. However, the V2R gives stronger emphasis to the relevance of shocks, trends and seasonality (known as the 'vulnerability context' in the Sustainable livelihoods framework), drawing on experience from disaster management and climate change work, to bring in a more detailed analysis of hazard exposure and the infrastructure, organization and governance context required to reduce such risks.

Disaster management

Approaches to disaster management – typically the domain of humanitarian agencies or humanitarian divisions of larger governmental or non-governmental agencies – have tended to focus on four areas: prevention, preparedness, response and recovery/reconstruction. These areas of activity are all directly related to hazard exposure – potential or actual – that can result in disaster. Other models, particularly the Pressure and Release (PAR) model (see **Section 4.1.2**) developed by Wisner et al. (1994), give greater recognition to the underlying causes of vulnerability to disaster, rooted in social and economic factors, rather than purely physical exposure.

The V2R approach highlights the importance of disaster prevention and preparedness in reducing disaster risk, thus reducing the need for response and recovery as disasters are reduced. It emphasizes that prevention and preparedness should be integrated within all livelihoods work, as the poor are most likely to live in hazard-prone environments. Disaster recovery and reconstruction must also aim to move beyond the immediate rebuilding of infrastructure and services in order to rebuild livelihoods in such a way that they will be less vulnerable in the future. A failure to make this link can leave people more vulnerable after a disaster than they were beforehand. Finally, the V2R approach builds upon the PAR model in seeking to address the underlying institutional, structural and ideological factors that contribute to vulnerability.

Climate change

Early work on climate change focused on understanding the possible changes that would take place in climate and weather, and the impacts that these would have on the physical environment. Much of the attention in terms of action was directed towards climate change mitigation – preventing further global warming by reducing carbon dioxide and other greenhouse gas emissions. However, in the past few years there has been a shift towards understanding the impacts of climate change on the poor better as well as the actions they need to take to adapt to those changes (Ensor and Berger, 2009; Strengthening Climate Resilience Project).

Climate change is leading to an increase in the frequency and severity of hazards and stresses, with detrimental effects on livelihoods, and an increasing frequency of disasters. In addition climate change impacts bring gradual changes to seasonal patterns and stresses such as pests and diseases that directly affect livelihoods, especially farming, and which are perhaps too complex for those who are most vulnerable to understand. Facing this uncertainty about what the future might bring, people struggle to adapt to the changes in their environment. The relevance of livelihoods and disaster management approaches to understanding and addressing the impacts of climate change is therefore becoming increasingly clear.

The V2R approach highlights the vital importance of understanding and addressing the ways in which climate change, and other long term trends (economic, socio-political or environmental for example), impact on poor people's vulnerability over time by undermining their livelihoods and increasing their exposure to hazards or stresses. It prioritises building the adaptive capacity of vulnerable people so that they have the assets, resources and capacities to respond not only to present threats, but also to potential, as yet unknown challenges, in the future.

Advancing practice

The V2R recognizes and draws on the experiences of different sectors as well as on the lessons from each of the above approaches. It also recognizes the work that has already been done to advance the integration of approaches. Integration of disasters and livelihoods thinking has taken great strides in recent years, as illustrated by Disaster Resistant Sustainable Livelihoods (ITDG, 2005), see **Section 4.1.3,** and Characteristics of a Disaster Resilient Community (Twigg, 2007) to name two examples. Within the last year, several useful models and frameworks to integrate climate change into both disaster and livelihoods work have been developed, particularly by non-government organizations (Pasteur, 2010). The V2R has been field-tested in a range of contexts and reviewed by international staff, leading to the inclusion of many examples from our own field-based practice.

1.3 A MULTI-LEVEL APPROACH

The V2R framework sets out key areas for analysis and action to address the diverse factors that contribute to vulnerability. Whilst communities should play a lead in the process of analysis, issues and stakeholders beyond the local level should be included. Furthermore, action to address vulnerability and to strengthen resilience must bridge the gaps between the local (micro), district or provincial (meso) and national or international (macro) levels.

Working with communities

The V2R provides a framework for a community-centred approach to reducing vulnerability. It recognizes the need to build the capacity of community members and institutions to analyse their situation and to plan and implement relevant activities to strengthen resilience. It is important for external stakeholders to build local capacity at all stages so that processes of analysis, planning and implementation can be community led and can be sustained and repeated without external support in the future. Communities are highly knowledgeable about their own environment and may have already developed local strategies for prediction, early warning, preparedness and coping which have evolved over long periods of time. They are also likely to be aware of the local resources and capacity available for taking action. A community driven process will lead to more effective and realistic analysis, plans and action than those developed by outsiders.

Inclusion of marginalized groups

Within any community there are likely to be groups who are marginalized or disadvantaged in some way and who may require particular attention to ensure that they are included. Groups are often excluded from participating on the basis of age, race, caste, gender, religion or other ethnic grounds. Sometimes people are unable to participate such as the disabled, the aged, the young or the very poor who may have other priorities and cannot prioritise participating in meetings over their immediate needs. These groups must be considered and specific actions taken to ensure that their views are incorporated in any analysis activities which take place in the community. These groups are often particularly vulnerable as a direct result of their limited voice in decision-making which could affect them. The young, old and disabled are also likely to face particular challenges in responding when hazards occur, they may not be able to move fast or a deaf person may not hear when an alarm is being raised.

Working with other stakeholders to achieve impact at scale

A community-based approach does not mean that action should only be focused at the community level. Whilst important analysis and action may take place at the community level, changes in organizational policy and practice are also needed to bring about long lasting and widespread change. Community perspectives on disaster risk reduction should be fed up into all other levels of decision-making – local, national and global. Communities can be empowered to access and influence relevant bodies to make their needs and priorities known, through a variety of channels, as will be discussed in **Section 2.6**. Practical Action's working model for achieving impact at scale (see **Section 4.1.4**) provides a framework for ensuring that projects and programmes achieve maximum impact by working at various levels to achieve change, including changing policies and practices.

PART 2

UNDERSTANDING THE V2R FRAMEWORK

2.1 INTRODUCTION

Disasters do not result from hazards alone, but from the impact of hazards on vulnerable communities, people with fragile livelihoods, for example, and who are inadequately prepared. Therefore, disasters are not inevitable and communities do not have to be helpless. Action can be taken to build resilience to hazards and strengthen capacity to adapt to longer term changes. But what exactly do we mean by the terms 'vulnerability', 'disaster' and 'resilience'? This section provides an introduction to the V2R framework, and explains some of the key terms.

What makes people vulnerable?

Vulnerability is **the degree to which a population or system is susceptible to, and unable to cope with, hazards and stresses, including the effects of climate change.** The causes of vulnerability are multi-dimensional. Vulnerability can be understood in terms of physical exposure to specific hazards: people are vulnerable to flooding when they live in low lying areas or on river banks; they are vulnerable to earthquakes when they live in areas with unstable plate tectonics. Vulnerability is also understood as being connected with social and economic conditions relating to people's livelihoods – few or fragile resources, low caste or class, poor education, lack of savings and so on. Livelihoods conditions often underlie physical exposure to threats as poor people are forced to live and work in unsafe locations because their options are limited. These conditions also make them more susceptible to the impacts of hazards meaning that fragile resources are more easily damaged and with few savings to draw on it is harder to respond effectively and recover promptly.

Vulnerability is increased by the wider context of uncertainty created by climate change and other long terms trends which are often not well understood by poor people. Furthermore, if people have weak access to, and influence over, the institutions and policies that govern their access to resources and decision making, they can do little to address the underlying causes of their vulnerability. These key elements that contribute to vulnerability are illustrated in Figure 2.

Vulnerability outcomes

When people with fragile livelihoods live in areas exposed to hazards they are vulnerable to disasters. Disaster is a relative term, but is commonly defined as **a serious disruption of the functioning of a community or a society involving widespread human, material, economic or environmental losses and impacts, which exceeds the ability of the affected community or society to cope using its own resources.** In all of the countries where Practical Action works there are communities who experience disasters. Excessive monsoon rains in Bangladesh in 2007 left

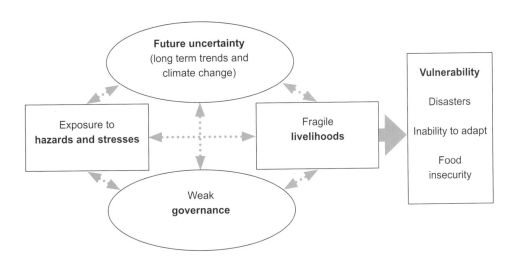

Figure 2. Vulnerability framework

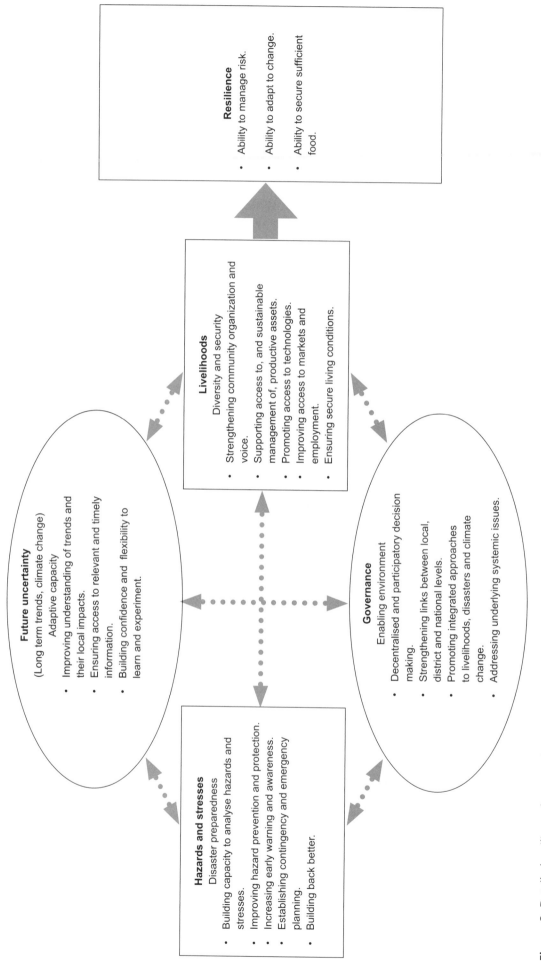

Figure 3. Detailed resilience framework

many people without homes and destroyed their harvests. The earthquake in Ica, Peru in August 2007 left hundreds dead and over a thousand injured. Drought in Northern Kenya in 2009 left many pastoralists destitute as their animals died of hunger.

Other hazards and stresses lead to outcomes that are not readily identified as disasters, but have negative outcomes, such as food insecurity, or halting people's progress out of poverty. Rampant inflation in Zimbabwe during 2008 meant that huge sectors of the population were unable to buy sufficient food and basic necessities. In North Darfur, Sudan, unreliable rains often lead to poor harvests resulting in seasonal periods of hunger, low cash income from crop sales and an inability to invest in improving wellbeing, for example health, education and housing. Long term trends, such as climate change, globalization and environmental degradation create new uncertainties for poor communities and they struggle to adapt to changes that result from these trends, imposing further stress on their livelihoods.

However, vulnerability is not a permanent state and communities are certainly not helpless in the face of hazards that might affect them. Even when severe hazards occur, these negative outcomes are not inevitable. Communities and individuals have skills, capacities and opportunities which can be built upon to strengthen their resilience and ensure that they are able to cope with hazard, adapt to change, and move out of poverty.

Building resilience

Resilience refers to **the ability of a system, community or society to resist, absorb, cope with and recover from the effects of hazards and to adapt to longer term changes in a timely and efficient manner without undermining food security or wellbeing**. Resilience can be thought of as the capacity to endure shocks and stresses and bounce back; individuals or communities that can ride out the difficulties that life might bring without their overall situation deteriorating. Even when affected by significant hazard events, or by longer term negative trends, they must be able to recover or adapt their livelihoods and continue to improve their lives and move out of poverty.

Increasing people's resilience means addressing the factors that underlie their vulnerability as illustrated in Figure 3 (see also Figure 1 for simple resilience framework). Improving the diversity and security of their livelihoods means that they have more options available, and can chose to live or work in areas less exposed to hazards, or at least have more resources to draw on in order to cope and recover when they are affected by negative events. Being better prepared for hazards and stresses can significantly reduce exposure. Improved understanding of long term trends, including climate change, means that people can draw on their available resources in appropriate ways in order to adapt to such changes over time. And finally, by creating a more enabling governance environment then people will be able to access or influence processes of decision making, service provision, and resource allocation.

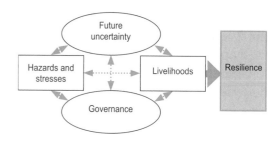

2.2 RESILIENCE OUTCOMES

What does resilience look like in practice? What outcomes are we aiming to achieve through the process of building resilience? This section explores different elements of resilience as an outcome: an ability to manage risks, to adapt to change, to secure sufficient food and to move out of poverty.

Ability to manage risks

An ability to manage risks includes the ability to understand and reduce the occurrence of hazards and stresses where possible, and when they cannot be prevented, to ride through the difficult period and to promptly rebuild or recover what they have lost. Positive coping strategies are an important aspect of resilience. These are **the strategies that households and communities use, based on available skills and resources, to face, manage and recover from adverse conditions, emergencies or disasters in the short term.**

It is important to note that not all coping strategies are positive. Vulnerable people are often forced to draw on strategies which erode their productive assets (for example selling them off or consuming them) and ultimately undermine livelihoods in the long run. Some erosive coping strategies are not easily detected, such as eating less and eating food of lower nutritional value, forgoing medical treatment or other such expenditures, and overexploiting natural resources.

Resilient households or communities pursue coping strategies which draw on excess, or liquid assets which have been stored up or saved for just such an eventuality (for example additional livestock, food stores or cash savings). Although this may diminish the total stock of assets, it will not undermine the future continuation of their livelihood. Therefore, once the period of exposure to stress or experience of disaster has passed and normal life has resumed, these assets can be rebuilt, replenished or repaid with relative ease.

Table 1. Erosive and non-erosive coping strategies

Vulnerability leads to erosive coping strategies, such as	Resilience leads to non-erosive, or positive coping strategies, such as
• Selling productive livestock, for example working animals or breeding animals. • Eating very little or very unpleasant foods resulting in weakening physical health. • Selling agricultural or fishing equipment. • Mortgaging or selling land • Borrowing money at very high interest rates • Over-exploiting natural resources	• Selling excess animals • Consuming less expensive or less preferred food, or gathering wild foods. • Drawing on kinship transfers of food or money, or reciprocal labour exchange • Selling non-essential possessions • Casual local work or temporary migration • Drawing on existing savings

Ability to adapt to change

A further outcome of resilience is the ability to adapt over the long term to changes which contribute to uncertainty, including environmental, political, economic, and importantly, climatic changes. Resilient households and communities are able to respond to change proactively, making active choices about alternative livelihood strategies that will maintain wellbeing under the changed context. This requires access to a diversity of livelihood assets, skills, information and institutional support which can be combined to expand the range of options and opportunities for responding to change.

Climate change adaptation refers to **the adjustment in natural or human systems in response to actual or expected climatic stimuli or their effects, which moderates harm or exploits beneficial opportunities**. Adaptive strategies differ from coping strategies. The latter are reactive, usually short term, strategies used by people to cope with hazards in the immediate term. Climate change adaptation relates to longer term, anticipatory strategies in which people adjust the ways in which they use their resources in order to explore new livelihood opportunities which internalize climate variability or other types of change.

Ability to secure sufficient food

Securing basic needs such as food is an important outcome related to resilience. It means that **households, and all members within them, are able to produce, purchase, or obtain sufficient, nutritious and culturally appropriate food at all times**. Vulnerable households often suffer food shortages as they are unable to produce enough to see them through the year and are also more adversely affected by adverse weather events. Reduced food intake (quality and quantity) can affect health, wellbeing and ability to work, which in turn can feed back to increase vulnerability. Resilience means being able to pursue safe and sustainable strategies to secure enough food throughout the year – without suffering seasonal shortages in the weeks or months leading up to harvest, as stored reserves run low. It also means being able to acquire food even when severe hazards, such as major flood or drought, occur, for example by having stored reserves, cash to purchase, or support from family or relief institutions.

Moving out of poverty

Households can quickly be pushed back into poverty by hazard events, or by unexpected changes in the climate. Resilient households are able to recover promptly from hazards, and adapt effectively to long term trends, and are therefore able to use their resources effectively to step out of poverty as Figure 4 illustrates.

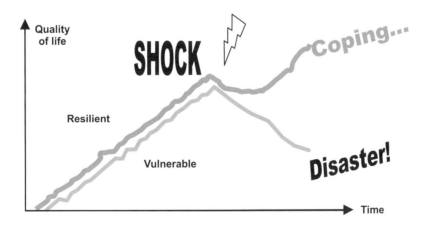

Figure 4. Resilience and moving out of poverty

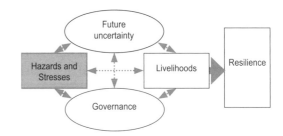

2.3 HAZARDS AND STRESSES

What kinds of hazards and stresses can push households or communities into crisis? What can be done to reduce the exposure of people and their livelihoods to such hazards and stresses? This section looks at a range of different types of hazards and stresses and their causes. It details four key areas of action to ensure that people understand the hazards and stresses that might affect them, and have taken relevant steps to prevent them, or where they are unavoidable, prepare for them.

What are hazards and stresses?

Hazards and stresses come in many forms. Hazards tend to be perceived as sudden onset, unexpected, high impact events such as earthquakes and cyclones. However, hazards can also include slow onset events such as creeping drought and small scale incidents such as a localized land slide. Other events which are seasonal in nature or which have less immediately noticeable impacts, can also seriously erode livelihoods, but may not be identified by people as hazards. We call these 'stresses' to ensure that they too are taken into account.

A hazard can be defined **as a dangerous phenomenon, human activity or condition that may cause loss of life, injury or other health impacts, property damage, loss of livelihoods and services, social and economic disruption, or environmental damage.** Stresses refer to **smaller, low impact events and seasonal factors, including unemployment, price fluctuations, ill health, local conflicts, or gradual changes in climate, which can undermine livelihoods.**

Table 2. A typology of hazards and stresses	
Atmospheric Heavy rainfall Hail / snowfall / blizzard High winds / hurricanes Extreme temperatures	**Geological** Earthquakes Volcanoes Landslides
Hydrological Floods Drought Cyclones	**Biological** Human epidemics (HIV and Aids) Plant pest outbreaks Animal disease outbreaks
Technological Oil spillage Radiation Infrastructural accidents (building / bridge collapse)	**Socio-political** Conflict War Land evictions Riots
Economic Exchange rate crises Hyper-inflation	

Table 2 illustrates that there are many different sources of shocks and stresses. Some hazards are caused by geophysical processes, such as earthquakes, or normal climatological patterns, such as regular monsoon rains. The causes of these events are beyond human control. However, many hazards are heavily influenced by human factors – both directly and indirectly – that either create hazards or make existing hazards worse. These are known as complex hazards. Human influence may be more obvious in the case of technological and financial hazards, for example poor construction of homes or bridges or inappropriate economic decisions.

However, many natural hazards are often partly human induced. Environmental degradation, such as deforestation, can contribute to the more severe effects of flooding or the occurrence of landslides, as there is no ground cover to slow the flow of water over the land. Conflict is another contributor to complex hazards. Conflict can turn low rainfall into famine. More than 50 per cent of Africa's food crises can be explained by armed conflict and the resulting displacement of populations (Green, 2008). Climate change is another human induced-factor that is exacerbating many existing hazards such as droughts and flooding. Climate change is one amongst several long-term trends which affect the incidence of hazards and increase vulnerability. Further discussion of these aspects of uncertainty and additional areas of action are detailed in **Section 2.5.**

Why is disaster preparedness important to resilience?

The poor are disproportionately affected by hazards affecting their ability to permanently step out of poverty. More than half of disaster related deaths occur in low human development countries, even though only 11 per cent of people exposed to hazards live there (DFID, 2005). A livelihoods approach to reducing vulnerability looks in detail at hazards and stresses but takes care to understand how and why people and their livelihoods are exposed to and affected by such events. Poor people are often more exposed to hazards and stresses, due to lack of knowledge or lack of choice; and they are usually more severely affected when hazards and stresses occur because they do not have the capacities and resources to cope.

The remainder of this section describes five areas of action which can help reduce households' and communities' physical exposure to hazards and stresses and increase their disaster preparedness.

- building capacity to analyse hazards and stresses;
- improving hazard prevention and protection;
- increasing early warning and awareness;
- establishing contingency and emergency planning;
- building back better.

Case Study 1: A vulnerable household in Nepal

Buddi Bahadur Kumal (67) and his wife Sukmaya (59) live near the confluence of Narayani and Rapti Rivers in Meghauli village, Chitwan district in south central Nepal. They have six children of which only one daughter still lives with them. Before Practical Action began to support activities to strengthen community resilience in their area, they were vulnerable in a number of ways.

The Kumal family has about one third of a hectare where they have a small hut, cultivate crops and keep small livestock (goats). Production from their land hardly meets heir food needs for six months of the year. As well as working on their own plot, planting, weeding and harvesting, Sukmaya also has to earn cash by labouring for others. Buddi fell from a tree in 1988 when he was collecting fodder, breaking his leg above the knee, and is now unable to work.

Wildlife encroachment from the nearby national park can destroy up to 80 per cent of crops during a bad attack. Prevention required mounting a 24-hour guard from seed sowing to the harvest season. Even the human population was at risk of attack: two villagers had been killed by rhinos. Potential livelihood options such as higher value vegetables and fruits were at greatest risk of theft by both animals and neighbours so they stopped cultivating them.

The land and house were exposed to flooding from the two big rivers which often flood during the monsoon season between June and August. In 2003 the family lost grains, blankets, kitchen utensils and four chickens to flooding. During floods, drinking water also became a problem as the community hand pump was affected by sediment build up.

Lack of water for irrigation is another stress they are increasingly facing. The family was unclear why water availability had reduced. They lacked the necessary skills to grow different crops. They also lacked the confidence to take risks and explore alternative ideas for income generation.

Credit: Practical Action Nepal

Buddi Bahadur Kumal outside his home in Chitwan, Nepal

2.3.1 Building capacity to analyse hazards and stresses

Vulnerable people often lack a good understanding of hazards or stresses and their associated risks, or of any action they could be talking to prevent or prepare for such threats. An important component of strengthening resilience is building community capacity for analysing and understanding the hazards and stresses that affect their lives as a first step towards taking action to address those hazards. Often, a lack of relevant skills, time or organizational capacity mean that a systematic analysis does not take place. As a result, whilst individuals may take personal action, there is little coordinated community action to reduce hazard risks and improve preparedness and response. Improving capacity for hazard assessment can be achieved by working directly with communities to carry out a systematic analysis and by providing training to community leaders to give them the skills to facilitate community analysis. However, to ensure sustainability and scale, it may be more appropriate to develop the skills of relevant district authorities to facilitate this process of community training and analysis.

Why is analysing hazards and stresses important?

There are many factors to think about when looking at different hazards and stresses so that communities can identify and prioritise key areas of action to reduce their impact.

Frequency/duration/seasonality/trends. In order to better understand and prioritise hazards and stresses it is useful to understand their frequency and duration. Some high impact hazards, such as the Asian tsunami in 2004, may leave a lasting impact on people, but these are infrequent. Addressing more frequent events may be prioritised if people take this factor into their decision-making. Many hazards and stresses are seasonal in nature, such as flooding, frosts, pest outbreaks, unemployment and low crop prices. When poor people do not have the means to cope with seasonal stresses, this is often what pushes them into destitution. It is important to consider how identified hazards and stresses are changing over time: whether they are becoming more or less frequent and how this relates to wider factors such as climate change (**see Section 2.5**).

Speed of onset/early warning. Some hazards occur without any warning at all and are very rapid in their impact such as an earthquake or a bridge collapsing. Others are more easily predicted as they arrive slowly or build up over several days or weeks, such as a cyclone or a disease outbreak. Others are very gradual and can remain almost unnoticed until they become critical, for example creeping drought, the build up of pollution and even some types of conflict. It is important to explore whether or not early warning systems exist. These might include formal structural systems such as early warning towers, as well as biophysical signals based on traditional knowledge — migratory patterns of birds, changing winds or flowering of certain plants, for example.

Underlying causes. As noted earlier, many hazards and stresses, even apparently 'natural' events such as flooding and drought, are in fact complex, with underlying human causes. To effectively address these hazards requires analysis of their underlying causes, which are often closely linked to the livelihoods practiced within the community; particularly those based on natural resources (**see Section 2.4.2**). Deforestation for wood fuel, cultivation or construction on steep slopes, for example, are frequent underlying causes of drought, flood and landslides and can be addressed within the community. In some cases communities are aware of the causes of hazards but do not have the resources, the skills or the influence to address them, for example unsustainable upstream infrastructure development. In other cases, the causes of hazards are long term trends that are not visible to or well understood by, the community, such as climate change or financial trends (**see Section 2.5**).

Scale, severity and focus of impact. Hazards and stresses can impact at a range of scales, from a limited group of households (for example a landslide), to multiple communities (such as the earthquake in Ica, Peru in 2005), or entire nations (like the seconomic crisis in Argentina in 2001-02).

An analysis of hazards and stresses should not focus only on the nature of the events themselves, but also seek to understand how they interact with communities and their livelihoods. Within any community, it is important to know which groups are affected most, whether these are groups practicing a particular livelihood (rain-fed farmers or fishermen, for example,), particular social groups (the young and old, women, people with disability), or people in a distinct geographical area (for example those living or working on riverbanks, or on slopes).

Community and individual resources affected. Hazards can damage or destroy resources that people rely on, whether those shared by the community, such as roads, schools, community buildings, water resources, etc, or those that are individually owned, for example land, homes, crops, etc. It is important to identify which resources are affected, how and why, in order to take steps to strengthen or protect them.

Action to build capacity for hazard analysis

In Zimbabwe Practical Action has been working through partner organizations to build capacity of communities in Gwanda district to identify and understand the critical hazards that contribute to their vulnerability. Drought is a regular phenomenon and was identified as an important hazard. However, veldt fires, a traditional practice of burning grassland to stimulate new pasture growth, were also raised as a seasonal problem as they often get out of control, burning beyond the intended area and destroying trees and homes. The identification of this hazard led to swift action to ensure that burning is carried out in a controlled way with oversight from a management committee.

Source: Practical Action Zimbabwe

Carrying out community vulnerability analysis, Gwanda District, Zimbabwe

2.3.2 Improving hazard prevention and protection

Hazards are often seen as a fixed element in the equation – as something we can do nothing to prevent or avoid. But many types of hazard, particularly those with underlying human causes, can be prevented, or at least reduced, for example by improving resource management and regulations. In other cases it is possible to physically protect people, homes and livelihoods from their impacts through various structural or regulatory measures.

Why are hazard prevention and protection important?

The costs of disasters can be huge, in terms of material losses as well as lives lost. In general the costs of prevention and protection are far less. During floods in Bangladesh in 1998 the value of cattle protected and saved by a four-acre flood shelter exceeded the cost of its construction by a factor of 17. But despite such statistics, it is still hard to get communities and governments to invest time and money in prevention activities. 'Building a culture of prevention is not easy. While the costs of prevention have to be paid in the present, their benefits lie in a distant future. Moreover, the benefits are not tangible; they are the disasters that did not happen' UN Secretary-General Kofi Annan in 1999 (cited in Green 2008).

Four interrelated areas of action can be investigated to improve hazard prevention and protection. Many of these actions are closely related to livelihoods, examined in more detail in **Section 2.4**, and to the governance context, addressed in **Section 2.6**.

Natural resource management. Human activity tends to disrupt the natural regulatory processes of the environment. For example, clearance of vegetation results in rain or flood water flowing fast over land without being absorbed, damaging soils through erosion, or sweeping away homes and other infrastructure in more extreme cases. Growing monoculture crops permits the build up of pests and diseases in the plant population leading to severe losses. Reduction of coastal mangroves results in seawater incursion. Managing natural resources as part of secure and diversified livelihoods (**see Section 2.4.2**) can therefore address the underlying cause of many hazards. Measures might include: maintaining vegetation, particularly on sloping land, for example through agroforestry practices; maintaining biodiversity (crops and animals) within the farm system; or managing grazing at sustainable levels.

Regulatory mechanisms. Poor planning and regulatory systems, relating to a whole range of issues, can result in increased risk. Housing or other infrastructure developments are often allowed to expand unchecked into hazard-prone areas and unregulated construction can lead to failure when put under pressure by hazard exposure. For example, inadequate storm water drainage, water supply and waste management can lead to unsanitary conditions during flooding and can exacerbate the flood impacts. Land use planning can help to control human activities in hazard prone areas. This requires effective enforcement, by raising awareness of the reasons for zoning and offering people alternative, safer options. Legal frameworks such as building codes, labour standards, pollution limits, and so on also help reduce hazard risk. Effective implementation of these regulatory mechanisms is often dependent on an enabling governance environment, which is discussed further in **Section 2.6**.

Structural measures. Where it is not possible to prevent a hazard, its physical effects are often devastating. Structural measures are important with respect to physical protection from hazards. Dykes, walls and bunds are often used effectively to protect land from flood waters. In Nepal, electric fencing has been used to keep elephants and other wild animals off farm land, preventing huge losses from damage. Appropriate building techniques can also help ensure that homes and other infrastructure can withstand shocks. Earthquake resistant and flood resistant housing are promoted by Practical Action in Peru and Bangladesh respectively, which incorporate structural measures to improve their endurance.

Social measures. Some hazards are enhanced by particular patterns of social behaviour. Social measures include raising awareness and encouraging dialogue around potential hazards to bring about changes in behaviour to help reduce their occurrence or impact. Examples include familiarising people with the use of bed nets to protect them from malaria, raising awareness about the transmission of HIV and Aids, or establishing peace committees to resolve tribal conflict.

Action to improve hazard prevention and protection

In Sri Lanka, much damage is done by unregulated development resulting in increased risk for the poor, as well as wasted resources and more frequent conflicts. Practical Action South Asia have developed two methodologies to promote improved assessment and planning processes within the formal government system to reduce disaster risk. The first of these is a Disaster Impact Assessment which should be carried out alongside an Environmental Impact Assessment during the planning stage of any significant infrastructure development. The second is Disaster Risk Sensitive Land Use Planning, which promotes a cross boundary approach to development planning. The process involves working with local authorities to develop localized hazards maps which are then superimposed onto existing land use maps to identify hazard prone areas. Further analysis is carried out with communities to identify physical, social, economic and environmental aspects of vulnerability. This information is then used by local planners to guide decisions about structural and agricultural developments.

In Nepal, practical steps have been taken in communities with which Practical Action is working to protect themselves from different hazards and stresses. Communities have reforested sloping lands and river banks, and built gabions (wire baskets filled with stones) to reduce river erosion resulting from flooding. With support from the National Park Authority, electric fencing has been installed along the borders between the Chitwan National Park and neighbouring communities to prevent the encroachment of wild animals which destroy crops and attack people.

Source: Practical Action Nepal

Gabion construction for flood protection in Kolhuwa, Nepal

2.3.3 Increasing early warning and awareness

Often there are warning signs well ahead of a hazard event. Weather forecasters observe the start of hurricanes and storms and can calculate their likely future strength and tracks; ecologists keep a watch on conditions that favour locust breeding; drought experts estimate the chances of rains. Communities also often have traditional ways of predicting or receiving warning of hazard events, for example watch towers to look out for wild animals or changes in wind direction which may signal certain types of weather.

Why are early warning and awareness important?

If warning can be given of an impending hazard event, then action can be taken to reduce the impacts on people and their belongings. What is important, therefore, is the ability to monitor or access the relevant warning information and to communicate that information to everyone who may be affected. Establishing an effective early warning requires communities to bring together information about known hazards, patterns and trends in their occurrence, and existing knowledge of early warning systems. This information should be collated during the process of hazard analysis as discussed in **Section 2.3.1**. Also, to be effective, there need to be plans in place and capacity built for the community to respond to the warning system. This will be looked at in **Section 2.3.4**. The elements we are interested in are the monitoring and warning system itself and the process of dissemination and communication.

Accessing monitoring and warning information. This might involve developing a hazard monitoring system within the community, or liaising with monitoring and early warning services outside the community. Community based systems of hazard monitoring include measurement of river levels (flood); assessments of seasonal food availability (famine); observation from watch towers (animal incursion); and reporting arrival of unknown livestock owners (pastoralist conflict). Other agencies can also provide relevant early warning information, such as national meteorological and hydrological services; specialized observatory and warning centres (for example for water, volcano); research institutes; extension services providers; and UN agencies such as UNISDR, WMO, FAO, UNESCO, UNEP, UNOSAT, OCHA. The important factor is establishing the mechanisms through which communities can access this information in timely and appropriate ways (for example through phone calls, radio broadcasts or personal visits). Furthermore, the information needs to be relevant to the local context, and in language and terminology that communities can understand and act upon.

Dissemination and communication. It is vital to communicate risk information and early warnings in a clear and timely manner to all those in the community for whom it is relevant. It is essential that systems are able to reach the poorest who are often least well connected, or may live in more remote areas. The warning information must be clear and useable, leading to appropriate response by those who hear it. This can be achieved with tools such as sirens, drums, phones, public announcements (loud hailer, radio, TV), door to door messaging, or any other practical measure that works within the particular context. Clearly the public need to be aware in advance of any emergency, how they should respond to an early warning message. This is dealt with in the next section.

Action to increase early warning and awareness

Nepal ranks as one of the most naturally risk prone countries in the world. Practical Action has been working on disaster mitigation in Nepal since 2001, particularly in reducing vulnerability to flash floods in the lowland Terai. Traditionally early warning towers have been used to keep watch for flash floods and incursion of wild animals as local communication possibilities were limited. Work was done to introduce higher and sturdier towers which gave a wider field of view and a greater range to sirens. However, telecommunications have improved in recent years and now an

Testing the early warning system in Nepal

effective system has been introduced whereby communities upstream monitor the river level and once it reaches a certain height then downstream communities, police and emergency services are alerted by mobile phone. In all locations electric sirens have been established, reliant on battery and 'inverter' systems due to the unreliability of mains power supply during heavy rains. Beyond the range of the siren communities have established different dissemination systems in each location, dependent on settlement patterns and geography. In all locations, cheap, simple hand microphones have been provided so that information can be broadcast, enabling specific messages to be communicated.

In Peru, Practical Action has been involved in working in schools to raise awareness about hazards and how to respond when they occur. Working with school children is a strategy for reaching the whole household as the children are encouraged to share what they have learned with their family as well as developing popular communications such as theatre or songs to spread appropriate messages in their communities. Practical Action has also worked with government at various levels to develop appropriate curriculum content which covers general issues around hazards, their underlying causes and how to reduce their probability (for example reforestation to reduce the risk of landslides and floods), as well as carrying out drills of what to do in the case of emergency, particularly earthquakes which affect large areas of the country. Educating the young has been found to be an effective way to bring about longer term change in hazard reduction and response behaviour.

2.3.4 Establishing contingency and emergency planning

Hazards vary considerably in their speed of onset and predictability. Vulnerability is increased when there is little warning of an impending hazard event meaning that people are unable to take action and move themselves or their belongings out of danger, for example. People are also more vulnerable when they do not have a plan of how to respond when hazards occur. In the case of sudden onset hazards, they may panic and behave in unsafe ways, or may not think to assist other members of the community to reach safety. If a community lacks safety equipment or medical supplies then they will also be unable to respond effectively or treat injured people. In the case of slow onset stresses, such as drought, a lack of planning can leave some households destitute, for example when crops fail.

Why is contingency and emergency planning important?

There are many actions which households and communities can take to improve their level of preparedness which will help keep their exposure to a minimum and ensure that they can respond swiftly and safely. Many forms of preparedness are more effective when the whole community works together to plan the actions to be taken before, during or in the aftermath of a hazard event. Emergency or contingency plans are important so that all members of the community know what to do and how to respond when hazards occur. An emergency plan is not the same as an overall disaster risk reduction plan – it is one element of this wider plan which should also include proposals for strengthening livelihoods and preventing hazards. Emergency or contingency planning should be based on a participatory community hazard analysis, which would identify who and what is most affected when hazards occur as outlined in **Section 2.3.1**.

Clearly, an emergency or response plan will differ according to the types of risks within the community, however it might include any of the following elements:

- Evacuation routes and safe locations that could be used as gathering places.
- Responsibilities allocated for ensuring vulnerable groups are attended to.
- Emergency shelters (temporary or permanent) for humans and livestock.
- Basic medical and first aid equipment, and people skilled to use them.
- Protection and rescue equipment, such as: shovels, ropes, boats, life jackets and so on.
- Emergency supplies (such as food, water, or the funds to purchase these).
- Communication systems and contacts for institutions that provide emergency services.

The plan should clearly outline different roles and responsibilities for people within the community and appropriate skills need to be built for those roles, for example medical training for first aiders. Some external funds may be needed to acquire necessary equipment, but well organized communities can meet many needs using their own resources, for example establishing an emergency fund, or coordinating contribution to an emergency food supply. Strengthening livelihoods (**Section 2.2**) ensures that households and communities have additional resources that they are able to contribute to such funds or stores.

The list above illustrates that there is much that the community itself can do to prepare for emergencies; however, links to external support services may well be necessary in the case of more extreme events. Establishing links with such organizations is important in order to raise awareness of potential community needs, and to ensure that they will provide appropriate types of response when they are needed (also dealt with in **Section 2.6**).

Action to establish contingency and emergency planning

To help address community vulnerability to floods in Kamargani Union of Gaibandha District in Bangladesh, 17 people (11 male and 6 female) came together voluntarily to form a disaster management committee to serve their community. Members of Ashar Alo Unnayan Sangstha were provided with relevant training and equipment so that they would be able to take the lead in

Source: Practical Action Bangladesh

Rescue boat in action during the 2007 floods in Gaibandha, Bangladesh

planning and awareness-raising around disaster preparedness. During a period of extreme floods in 2007 the work of the committee swiftly implemented the emergency response plans they had set in place. As they had been monitoring the flood situation they were able to disseminate early warning messages and using boats they were able to quickly rescue flood marooned families. 'Our members rescued flood stranded people, shifted 23 lots of housing materials damaged by river erosion and constructed temporary cattle shelters for 75 cattle. We installed six temporary sanitary latrines and three elevated tube wells for people marooned in the flood shelters. We later repaired three culverts and organized two vaccination camps for the cattle' said Mohammad Sabu Mia, Secretary of the committee. 'This year's flood gave us an opportunity to test our plan and what we had learned from our training. I think we have passed the test.'

2.3.5 Building back better

After a disaster, reconstruction often fails to adequately support community and economic development – it deals better with the needs of elites than those of of the marginalized poor. Now the focus on reconstruction is turning to alternative, more participatory approaches, such as People-Centred Reconstruction (PCR). However, many agencies still struggle to put this into practice as there is relatively limited experience of PCR.

Why is building back better important?

In 1970, major earthquakes struck Peru and Turkey, causing much damage and many casualties. In both cases, the government initiated large reconstruction programmes, often involving relocation, and received assistance from external humanitarian agencies on an unprecedented scale. The approaches followed by governments and agencies alike were to build houses for people rather than with them. Evaluations have since highlighted that this approach doesn't work, and many of the houses built remained unoccupied, whilst those affected reverted to their old ways of building and remained vulnerable to future risks. This approach to reconstruction, which had agencies in the driving seat, is nowadays often called Donor-Driven Reconstruction (DDR). However, PCR includes everyone: house-owners, tenants and squatters and puts people and reducing their vulnerability at the centre of the process. PCR involves:

- empowering poor people through their participation in key decision-making processes from as early as possible;
- building back better against possible future risks;
- rebuilding livelihoods to enable people to recover assets and become more resilient (rather than long-term dependent).

The principles of PCR have been applied by Practical Action in two significant contexts: in Sri Lanka after the tsunami in 2005 and in Peru after the earthquake in Ica in 2008. The lessons learned helped to further refine the approach and have been widely disseminated. A process of PCR should include the following components:

- A detailed assessment of damage, needs, resources and capacities is needed. This happens in collaboration with the affected communities and all information is fully shared with everyone.
- Mobilization of communities for participatory planning, including Community Action Planning (CAP) with the communities and other stakeholders, including local and national government institutions, utilities, NGOs and aid agencies needs to happen. Particular attention needs to be paid to including the demands of the most vulnerable. Prioritisation is important too, to match planned actions to the resources that can be accessed by the partners.
- Participatory housing design with communities should pay attention to safer construction and local sustainability (see **Section 2.4.5**).
- Supportive measures for PCR need to focus on increasing people's resilience, including developing and strengthening livelihoods and community-based savings and credits.
- Support for construction is important, such as:
  - selecting and training builders to support households;
  - promoting production of local building materials or bulk-buying of materials from elsewhere, to reduce costs;
  - constructing infrastructure to service houses;
  - providing cash for reconstruction although some funding should be held back to support those needing more time to recover.

Some infrastructure can be constructed by local people through community contracts, which will help them to recover and retain money in the local economy.

Action to build back better

The tsunami of December 2004 devastated over two-thirds of Sri Lanka's coastline. More than 50,000 lives were lost and 100,000 households displaced along the eastern, southern and western coastlines. An estimated 120,000 houses were damaged or destroyed. Seventy-five per cent of the total fishing fleet was lost and close to 25,000 acres of arable land were affected by salinity. Overall 150,000 people lost their main source of livelihood. From January 2005 Practical Action worked with affected communities to reconstruct housing and to re-establish livelihoods, infrastructure, sanitation and health. Using context-specific participatory approaches, the communities were involved at all stages.

Over three years, around 160 homes were built using cost-effective appropriate building technologies. The houses were designed in cooperation with the owners. They were built in partnership with 13 local NGOs, and included six demonstration houses and one training building. Over 300 masons were trained in the building technologies. These were important strategies to promote local replication. The communities where Practical Action worked were also assisted in the devel-

Source: Lucy Stevens, Practical Action

Post tsunami reconstruction of housing in Sri Lanka

opment of income generation opportunities, either by replacing existing equipment for fishermen and weavers or by developing new opportunities. Secure and sustainable development was further promoted through rain-water harvesting tanks for domestic and agricultural use, community-based waste processing infrastructure and eco-sanitation, demonstrations of wind, solar and bio-gas energy systems, and preparation of disaster preparedness plans (World Habitat Awards, no date).

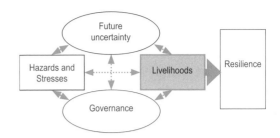

2.4 LIVELIHOODS

If households are to be resilient they need adequate resources (for example cash, food, local organizations and skills) to draw on in times of need. They also need livelihoods that are secure and not easily damaged by hazards and stresses. Having access to a diversity of resources is important for resilience. Natural resources in particular need to be well-managed to ensure that they do not contribute to the occurrence of hazards and stresses.

What are livelihoods?

A livelihood comprises **the resources (including skills, technologies and organizations) and activities required to make a living and have a good quality of life**. Understanding livelihoods does not mean just looking at people's main source of employment or income, but at all the different activities and choices within the household and community which provide food, health, income, shelter and other tangible and intangible benefits, such as comfort, safety, respect and fulfilment.

Livelihood activities can include agricultural production (crops, vegetables, livestock, fish) for home consumption or for sale of produce; non agricultural home production such as tailoring, pottery, food processing, and so on; wage employment locally or migrating to another area to work; or harvesting forest products. Activities such as caring for children and the elderly should also be recognized as important roles often played by women. The livelihood options available to individuals and households depends on the diversity of resources, skills and technologies they are able to access. The security of their livelihood also depends on the security of their available resources.

Why are livelihoods important to building resilience?

People with poor livelihood options are more likely to be forced into living or working in areas more exposed to hazards and stresses. When people are faced with extreme situations they may resort to livelihood activities which are dangerous or undesirable such as begging, illegal factory work, forest exploitation, or prostitution. In Bangladesh those who do not own land may have no other option but to exploit government owned, flood exposed river banks, risking eviction by authorities. When hazards do occur, people with fragile livelihoods tend to have little to draw on in such times of need, pushing them deeper into crisis. With limited resources they are likely to be dependent on one or two key sources of food and income. If these are affected in any way by an external shock then they will have little else to fall back on. Their ability to adapt to changed circumstances and pursue alternative livelihood strategies will be limited. Many poor households in Zimbabwe are dependent only on rain-fed agriculture, leaving them vulnerable if the rains are poor. Lacking financial capital they struggle to invest in other opportunities such as small livestock, which could provide them with an alternative source of income if a harvest fails.

With access to diverse, secure and well managed resources, resilient households can pursue a number of different strategies to provide food throughout the year, income for regular needs and to save for times of emergency. In this way they are often able to avoid exposure to hazards. When hazards are unavoidable, people with diverse livelihoods will be able to draw on a range of resources and skills to pursue positive coping strategies, ride through the difficult times, and continue to move out of poverty.

Livelihoods in relation to other aspects of the V2R framework. The V2R framework illustrates that livelihoods can be affected by hazards and stresses. To ensure livelihood security requires sound analysis of potential hazards and stresses and action to reduce their impact through disaster preparedness activities. In turn, many hazards and stresses result from certain livelihood choices (for example cultivation of steep slopes which can lead to landslides). Therefore promotion of sustainable livelihood options is essential to reducing such threats.

Long term trends, including climate change, introduce an element of uncertainty about the future viability of livelihoods. Long term trends can in turn be caused by unsustainable resource use such as deforestation. Such trends must also be considered in a vulnerability analysis and steps taken to better understand them, address them where possible, or strengthen capacity to adapt livelihoods when necessary (see **Section 2.5**). Finally, livelihoods are very often shaped by the wider governance environment. Policies and organizational practice determine how livelihood resources, skills and technologies can be accessed from outside the community. Again, there is a two-way relationship: communities should be able to make demands on the governance environment, and policies and organizations can be made more responsive to their needs (see **Section 2.6**).

Action to ensure diverse and secure livelihoods

Practical Action supports livelihoods by improving the diversity and security of resources, skills and technologies that are available to households and communities. This work is grouped under five areas which are explained in more detail in the following sections. They correspond roughly to the five assets of the sustainable livelihoods approach developed by DFID: social, natural, human, financial and physical (see **Sections 1.2** and **4.1**). Different aspects of these five areas may be addressed to differing degrees in different projects depending on the issues identified by the community.

- strengthening community organization and voice;
- supporting access to and management of natural resources;
- promoting access to skills and technologies;
- improving access to markets and employment;
- ensuring secure living conditions.

Case Study 2: Livelihood constraints in Coyllur, Peru

Practical Action works in the community of Coyllur, in the high Andes of Peru. The following is a description of their livelihood situation and some typical challenges people faced when Practical Action first started working there.

Most people practice small scale agriculture, growing maize, wheat, barley, peas, beans, potatoes and other tubers. Land holdings are very small (on average 2 hectares per family) which limits production. Most farmers are dependent on rainfall to irrigate their crops, though some are able to access water from irrigation channels on an intermittent basis. Water is a limited resource and has to be carefully managed. The short growing season and limited access to water means that only one crop can be grown per year. Livestock keeping is fairly minimal with small numbers of sheep, cattle, pigs and goats are kept in the higher reaches of the village and small animals such as guinea pigs, poultry and rabbits in the lower parts. Animal health has tended to be very poor due to the lack of support services, and people's inability to afford necessary vaccines. In Peru, public extension services were virtually eliminated during structural adjustment cuts in the 1990s. Production has been mainly subsistence based. Some food insecure months were faced due to low production and lack of financial resources to buy food when store food ran out.

Household income is typically low. Apart from agriculture people have had few other livelihood options. Some people sell vegetables and other excess crops in the market, but the road from the top of the community is poor and transport infrequent so reaching the market from there is expensive and therefore little profit is made on sales. Casual labour in the town pays a low wage and is not a desirable option as it takes the men from the community. Education levels are low as only basic primary schooling is available in the community. As a result of poor work and education opportunities, many people were leaving the community altogether. The local Mayor is dynamic and keen to lead local institutions in developing projects, but their capacity to develop proposals and to access financial resources has been weak.

Many families in the community of Coyllur in Peru have been affected by changing weather patterns over the past 5 or so years. Heavy frosts in particular have been coming out of season and killing off potato plants destroying any potential for a harvest of an important staple. Heavy rains cause landslides also destroying crops. More and more of the affected families were leaving the community to find work elsewhere. Those who are left were becoming demoralized about the future.

Credit: Practical Action Nepal

Don Gregorio struggles to produce a good harvest in a changing climate, Coyllur, Peru

2.4.1 Strengthening community organization and voice

Community organizations include Village Development Committees, women's organizations, church groups, farmer groups or cooperatives, health promotion groups, etc. Also known as Social Capital, these might be formal and recognized committees which are supported by government, or they may be informal in nature, self organized and self reliant in terms of resources. Local groups and organizations which have some basic skills for planning and resource mobilization can be extremely powerful in motivating community members to strengthen their resilience in various ways.

Why is community organization and voice important?

Poorly organized communities leave households isolated in terms of addressing their problems and needs. When households are affected by hazards they are often left feeling powerless. Long term trends can induce a similar response when they are poorly understood and beyond local control. This can create a vicious cycle of despondency leading to further inaction to address the causes of their problems. Working collaboratively, households can achieve more than when working alone to address the problems they face. They can:

- take the lead in analysing the causes of their vulnerability and creating plans to address them;
- invest resources and labour together to address specific local needs;
- establish and maintain structures to manage resources and resolve conflicts;
- have a greater voice in influencing external decisions or access institutions with better resources or services – in Peru local government, for example, has financial resources available for development activities, but communities lack the skills to develop funding proposals and so the resources often go unspent.

By building understanding, confidence, skills and motivation, communities can be empowered to work together to ensure they are better prepared for potential threats and trends and can respond effectively when they occur. Particularly vulnerable groups often exist who are excluded from community institutions on the basis of gender, caste, class or merely because they do not have time to participate (see **Issues Page 3: Gender**). Attention must be paid to ensure that community organizations include the poor and represent their needs.

Action to strengthen community organization and voice

The V2R approach aims to empower communities to take control over all aspects of their development, as well as to resist unfavourable forms of development. Practical Action works with community organizations in such a way as to achieve three important principles:

- facilitate empowerment and self-reliance;
- include and represent the poor;
- meet practical and strategic needs.

By working through community organizations, skills and ownership of all initiatives remain within the community, contributing to long term sustainability. A principal starting point is therefore to build community capacity to understand the causes of their vulnerability and to plan, organize and access resources to address those issues. This is critical to improving disaster preparedness (see **Section 2.3**), as well as to strengthening livelihoods. Alongside local planning and action, communities need to better understand and influence decisions and policies that affect their lives and livelihoods, and to demand fulfilment of their rights.

Strengthening community organizations is the key strategy used in northern Darfur, Sudan for helping people to help themselves. In the absence of any other local organizations, communities form a VDC or a Women's Development Committee (WDC) as a starting point for their engagement in activities to build resilience. These committees coordinate and manage Practical Action's support to strengthening and diversifying livelihoods and improving disaster preparedness, including training in drought-resilient farming practices, goat restocking, building stores to protect crops from pests, and establishment of grain banking systems to ensure seed is saved for replanting if a harvest is lost to drought. In order to ensure sustainability, the VDCs and WDAs charge a membership fee which is reinvested in managing local activities. For larger project fundraising, Practical Action has provided support and training to members of Village and Women's Development Networks (which represent the VDCs and WDAs) to help them submit proposals to other NGOs and international agencies. In 2008 the VDC Network reported securing funds for nine projects – including one funded by the UN Food and Agriculture Organization (FAO) for the sum of $300,000 for the blacksmith association to produce agricultural tools for free distribution. The WDA Network reported having around 11,000 members and eight funded projects (including goat restocking, sewing and food processing training), ranging from $5,000 to $210,000 (Coupe and Pasteur, 2009).

In North-west Kenya, the region bordering Ethiopia, Sudan and Uganda, recurrent drought and disease epidemics have decimated herds on which pastoralist tribes depend for their survival. This is leading to near continuous cattle raiding by neighbouring tribes, carried out by small groups of men with automatic weapons and driven by criminal motivation for profit. The results are devastating. It is estimated that cattle raids currently account for more than 70 per cent of deaths among males aged 30 to 39 in tribes that inhabit the region. Practical Action has helped establish two peace and grazing committees to fulfil the role of traditional institutions that have been weakened or ceased to exist. Both government and communities have recognized the committees as legitimate representatives on matters of conflict resolution and grazing management. Cross border peace meetings and dialogue between committees have yielded encouraging results. Stolen livestock have been traced and returned to their rightful owners in Uganda. This, in the opinion of local residents, could never have happened before. Herders from opposing tribes across the border were also reported to be sharing grazing areas and water sources without incident, a situation not seen in over 10 years.

Turkana herdsman with his camels, Kenya

Source: Georgina Cranston

2.4.2 Supporting access to and sustainable management of natural resources

Natural resources form the basis of the majority of rural communities' livelihoods, using them to produce food and other goods for consumption or sale. These could include land, forest, lakes and rivers, clay, and various types of animal and plant species for farming, forestry, fishing, production of non timber forest products, food processing, handicrafts and other rural livelihoods. Access to such resources is often essential for production in rural areas, and sustainable management ensure that livelihoods are secure and sustainable in the long term.

Why are access to and sustainable management of natural resources important?

Those who are most vulnerable tend to be people with poor access to natural resources upon which to build their livelihood strategies. With limited resources they are likely to be dependent on one or two key sources of food and income. If these are affected in any way by an external shock then they will have little else to fall back on. Their ability to adapt to changed circumstances and draw on alternative livelihood strategies will be limited. Unable to access water resources for irrigation, many poor households in Zimbabwe are dependent only on rain-fed agriculture, leaving them vulnerable if the rains are poor. Diversifying their resources, through investing in small livestock could provide them with an alternative source of income if a harvest fails.

Natural resource management is also necessary for the effective functioning of ecosystems from which people derive many benefits. Healthy ecosystems provide natural regulation of or defences against hazards, for example mangroves, dunes and reefs create physical barriers between communities and coastal hazards. They also provide the necessary nutrient inputs for food production and also provide cultural services such as spiritual, recreational, and cultural benefits. Natural resource degradation reduces the capacity of the environment to meet social and ecological objectives, and needs, and can lead to increased frequency and intensity of natural hazards.

Access to natural resources is often contested between different social groups. In northern Kenya, there are disputes between different pastoralist communities over grazing rights, compounded during dry years. These disputes have at times led to armed conflict creating a further hazard for those populations. Poor management of resources can reduce their productivity over the long term and can lead to increased hazard risk. In Nepal, for example, farmers who are only able to rent land on a short term basis are less inclined to manage soils for long term sustainability compared to those who own their land. Failing to invest in maintaining soil quality reduces its productivity and makes farmers more vulnerable to drought.

Natural resources need to be combined with other resources discussed in **Section 2.4** (community organization, skills and technologies, markets and so on) to maximize their use and achieve secure and diverse livelihoods. Community organization can help resolve conflict over resource access, appropriate skills and technologies can ensure that they are used productively, and access to markets is essential if a good income is to be earned which can then be reinvested in livelihood improvements and disaster preparedness measures.

Action to support access to and sustainable management of productive assets

Practical Action works with communities to help them to access resources, resolve conflicts and ensure that resources are managed in such a way that they are not degraded for future generations and continue to provide valuable ecosystem services. Secure access to productive resources is important for communities and households to be able to plan for their future and use their resources effectively and sustainably. In Nepal, for example, farmers have been assisted to rent land on a longer term basis and are now more inclined to invest in soil conservation. In Kenya, tribal conflict over access to grazing areas for their livestock has been reduced by creating dialogue around practical activities to improve resources such as livestock watering points. A consensus building approach used in Jamalpur, Bangladesh, has ensured equal access by rich and poor to communal fishing resources. A Water Body Management Committee was established to oversee appropriate management (restocking and limited harvesting) and to distribute profits equally. Taking active responsibility for the water body has meant that it is not overexploited by the members.

Growing a diversity of crops or crop varieties reduces risk from failure of one particular crop due to pests or drought. Agricultural diversification is particularly relevant in the context of climate change, as a diversity of crops can help ensure resilience to a wider range of weather patterns. Practical Action has done work to help farmers to rebuild crop and livestock biodiversity. Farmers in Tharaka in Kenya have traditionally grown a wide variety of grains for their different benefits: fast maturing, good taste, or high market price. However, after a number of severe droughts many of these varieties were lost. Farmers then planted the varieties which had been given to them as drought relief but which were not suited to the local soils and climate. These farmers have been assisted to revive many of their lost varieties through organizing seed fairs at which they display and exchange their seed – not only grains (millet, sorghum and maize), but also vegetables and legumes (such as pumpkin and mung bean). These fairs have continued to take place since the project ended eight years ago and farmers now say that they are once again growing a diversity of crops and that harvests are more secure as a result.

Source: Eric Kisiangani, Practical Action East Africa

Farmer exhibiting a diversity of varieties at a seed fair in Kenya

2.4.3 Promoting access to technologies

Vulnerable groups tend to lack access to appropriate technologies to help them to make best use of their available resources or to protect them from possible hazards. Ensuring that appropriate technologies for secure and diversified production are accessible to marginal producers is at the heart of Practical Action's approach. We define technologies as skills and knowledge, physical hardware such as tools or water points, and the way they are organized or combined. Appropriate technologies are those which are cost effective for small scale producers, which can be managed and maintained by them over the long term, and which integrate environmental, economic and social sustainability.

Why is access to technologies important for building resilience?

Appropriate technologies can help vulnerable producers to overcome the physical and environmental constraints of hazard prone areas, improve productivity and incomes and to help them adapt to changes in the climate. Poor farmers in Sudan with access to a donkey plough are able to work the good quality wadi soils and produce more food. Livestock keepers with access to extension or advisory services can improve their understanding of management or feeding strategies for their animals, and access vaccines, reducing their vulnerability to pest or disease outbreaks. Enhanced capabilities outside of farming mean that particularly women and young people are able to develop alternative livelihoods, such as pottery, food processing, or other types of craft, that can provide additional income or prove more resilient when agriculture is threatened by weather events. In the context of long term trends, including climate change, the ability to update knowledge and skills about the impacts of trends and new livelihood options is ever more important (see **Section 2.5**).

Action to promote access to technologies

Practical Action promotes access to a wide range of agricultural and non-farm skills and technologies to increase security, income and food. Technology diffusion and continuing innovation does not necessarily happen automatically. Promoting technology access is achieved in a range of different ways, from direct training to communities, to training local extension agents, improving linkages with other knowledge sources, such as government service providers, research organizations, the internet, etc., and improving the technology capabilities of rural people themselves to experiment and develop their own innovations (see **Issues Page 1**).

Extension services are an important channel for accessing improved agricultural production technologies. However, state run extension services are being phased out in favour of private sector providers, which tend not to reach dispersed farmers in remote areas, and are often oriented towards advice relating to sale of inputs rather than low external input technologies which may be more appropriate to resource poor farmers. Practical Action overcomes this gap working with the remaining government extension services to facilitate the training of community-based extension workers with skills in agriculture, horticulture, animal health and fisheries. Living in rural communities these extension workers are able to provide prompt and cost effective advice and support to their fellow farmers, charging a small fee for services or inputs provided. Established links with government, researchers and other service providers allows them to access and disseminate available technology options which improve production and reduce risk. Community Animal Health Workers, for example, are able to provide effective livestock vaccines which reduce the incidence of disease outbreaks. In Sudan, community agricultural extension workers alert government staff when there is a threat of locust attack, and they are then able to respond swiftly with localized pest control. There is potential for community extension workers to be an important conduit for evolving knowledge about climate trends and skills to help people to adapt to them.

Some technologies can increase production, but they also carry certain risks. The combined use of proprietary seeds, fertilizers and pesticides has been shown in many instances to lead to significant yield increases, particularly in the short term. However, requirements for up-front cash investment, access to input markets and credit, and higher levels of education, often make seed, fertilizer and pesticide packages less accessible to the poor. Furthermore, over-reliance on these external inputs, which can fluctuate in price and availability, also increases the vulnerability of small farmers, including their risk of indebtedness and the long-term degradation of the environment on which they depend. Practical Action favours low input, integrated agro-ecological approaches (see Table 3) that have been shown to be more suited to farming systems with higher labour availability, which encourage sustainable management of natural resources, and have proved to be more secure and productive in hazard environments. In Zimbabwe, mulching, intercropping and agro-forestry have proven to be successful and sustainable approaches to soil and pest management. In Bangladesh, floating gardens, constructed on rafts made of bamboo and water hyacinth, allow farmers to produce vegetables and rice seedlings before flood waters have receded, making production more secure even when flooding extends beyond its usual season.

Table 3. Technologies for sustainable and hazard resistant agricultural production	
Soil and water management • Terraces and other structures to prevent water runoff and erosion • Contour ridges • Manures and composting • Pit cultivation • Irrigation technologies • Earth dams *Pest and weed control* • Integrated pest management • Post harvest crop storage structures • Post harvest pest management and storage	*Seeds and tools* • Biodiversity for risk reduction • Seed selection and replication • Crop diversification (both modern and traditional varieties) • Donkey plough *Land management* • Floating gardens (Bangladesh) • Wadi cultivation (Sudan) • Back garden cultivation

Credit: Practical Action Bangladesh

Floating garden technology in Bangladesh

Issues Page 1. Technology for resilient communities

Practical Action sees technology as a vital contributor to reducing people's vulnerability and strengthening their livelihoods. Our definition of technology includes physical infrastructure, machinery and equipment as well as the knowledge and skills and the capacity to organize and use all of these. Simple, innovative ideas to help people change their lives for the better

Improvements to technologies can have many positive impacts for poor people's livelihoods. They can:

- Help producers to overcome the physical and environmental constraints of fragile areas, improve productivity and incomes, and to help them to adapt to changes in the climate.
- Ensure lower costs, for example, through labour saving devices such as a draught plough which will reduce labour costs.
- Help people to reach new markets through mobile phone or internet access to market information, for example.
- Protect people or assets from hazards - for example raised housing or dams can protect from floods, vaccinations can protect people and animals from health hazards.
- Enhance early warning of, and response to, hazards with sirens, rescue boats, life jackets and so on.

Whether modern or traditional, local or introduced, with access to a wider choice of technology options producers are able to innovate and improve their practices. Practical Action does not rule out any technologies on the grounds of ideology or dogma – we are in favour of any technology that can benefit the poor in a sustainable way. Since the 1980s we have used an approach called Participatory Technology Development (PTD) to facilitate farmer-driven technology innovation. More recently, this approach has further evolved into one of strengthening technology capabilities to help people to access, adapt, and make appropriate choices about available technologies.

Technology capabilities

Building technology capabilities is about enabling resource poor women and men to identify and develop technologies to address their needs as these needs change over time, to improve their ability to use and adapt technologies in response to a changing environment. This involves strengthening links with local research stations and other sources of new technologies; building confidence and skills to experiment, analysing and assessing technologies through field-based learning situations and exposure to new ideas; and ensuring capacity to manage and maintain technologies over time. Building such capabilities, rather than simply transferring technologies, is increasingly important in the context of climate change (see **Section 2.5**) as farmers in particular will need to adapt to new weather patterns over the long term.

Assessing technologies

Availability of a technology does not guarantee its use. It is important to assess the risks and benefits associated with different technology options in a systematic manner, both with poor people and with those that develop and control technologies. Promoting debate and discussion around the potentials and pitfalls of different technologies and the institutions that promote or control them is important. The following issues are relevant to assessing technologies, which can then be weighed up and discussed using a simple table as illustrated below (Table 4).

- Social: will the technology affect women differently from men? Is it acceptable and accessible to all social groups (religious, caste, age, etc)?
- Technical: do people have the knowledge or skills to use and maintain the technology?
- Environmental: is the technology likely to benefit or damage the environment, considering both the short and long term?
- Economic: are there market opportunities? Is the technology affordable to those who need it most?
- Institutional: how will the technology be managed to ensure long term sustainable use? Who has overall control of the technology?

Table 4. Tool for assessing technologies

	Risk / cost	Opportunity / benefit
Social		
Technical		
Environmental		
Economic		
Institutional		

Practical Action facilitated a farmer's jury in Zimbabwe in 2003 to help a group of farmers to explore the costs and benefits of different technology options, and how they related to their own vision for the future of agriculture in their country. In particular, debates were held around the introduction of Genetically Modified Organisms (GMOs) and the impact of Intellectual Property Rights (IPRs) on farmers' rights to access patented seed varieties. In 2007, Practical Action hosted exchanges between rural communities in Zimbabwe and scientists from the UK and Southern Africa to assess the risks and potential for nanotechnology in the field of rural water supply filtration.

Technology governance

Policies and institutions at various levels play important roles in facilitating or blocking appropriate technology access by the poor. States, for example, can provide positive incentives for pro-poor research and development. On the other hand international regimes (such as IPR) have tended to encourage the control of knowledge for private rather than public gain. Governance mechanisms (see **Section 2.6**) must include the voices of poor people both in policy setting and in the ongoing assessment of the impact of technology choices.

Practical Action has lobbied at an international level for changes to intellectual property laws that prevent small-scale food providers and communities from developing, saving, exchanging and selling seeds, livestock breeds and fish species. We also raise awareness amongst national governments about the types of technology choices that are pro-poor and environmentally sustainable. For example a national workshop organized in collaboration with partner NGOs, exposed the Bangladesh Ministry of Agriculture and scientists from a variety of research organizations to the model of ecological agriculture and associated production technologies.

2.4.4 Improving access to markets and employment

Markets are the arrangements by which people buy and sell goods and services, whether for money, through barter or by some other method of exchange. People need access to markets for inputs, infrastructure, services and consumption goods to improve their production and livelihoods. In turn they can sell produce for cash income. Sale of labour, through employment in a trade is also an important livelihood opportunity. For markets to function, a range of other players supporting the core buyers and sellers are relevant, as well as policies, regulations and customs that facilitate people's ability to trade. This total picture is called the market system.

Why is access to markets and employment important for resilience?

Access to markets is important both for the buying and selling of inputs, goods, services and labour. As a result of physical remoteness or lack of infrastructure vulnerable communities and producers often face constraints in accessing markets and are unable to purchase the necessary inputs, such as seed, animal vaccines, labour, tools or other materials, as well as for selling their produce at a good price. Lacking access to information on market demand, quality, prices and so on means they are unable to take advantage of new market opportunities to improve their livelihoods. Furthermore, local market prices for their crops are often undermined by imported food from countries where production has been subsidised. Market distortion is often greatest after a disaster when various forms of aid flood in and make it very difficult for those who have managed to produce a harvest to get a decent price.

With good access to output markets and employment producers can diversify their livelihoods and gain a cash income. Savings, whether in the form of cash, or other items (such as jewellery) which can be easily sold or exchanged, can constitute an important positive coping strategy to be drawn on in times of need. Loans and credit services are also important for facilitating access to financial resources for investing in new initiatives. Well functioning input markets can ensure that production can be maximized and security enhanced. When attention is paid to the impacts of disasters on markets, humanitarian or development organizations can tailor their response to ensure that markets continue to function in favour of local producers.

Action to improve access to markets and employment

In order to earn a sustainable income from their production it is important that farmers are able to engage effectively in markets which have the potential to improve their livelihoods. Practical Action's Markets and Livelihoods Team have developed a participatory and systemic approach to helping producers work with other market actors, such as traders and policy makers, to identify and address key market opportunities and constraints.

Participatory Market System Development is an approach to guide analysis and action for better functioning markets that are more open and inclusive. Participatory Market Mapping (Figure 5) is a key tool used to help producers and other market actors to understand blockages and opportunities. Market Mapping can help producers increase their understanding of the market system they are part of and it helps them to build connections and relationships with key actors such as service providers and buyers. Strengthening their understanding of the market and their relationships with buyers, for example, means they can make better decisions about what crops or products to produce – what is in demand, who other suppliers are, for example. From the analysis, issues are identified that require attention. Improving relationships and communication between producers and other market actors (traders, consumers, wholesalers, and so on) is important in order to overcome challenges that are limiting potential (for example quality or quantity of production). In the State of Kassala in Eastern Sudan, participatory market mapping helped groups of semi-nomadic pastoralists and other actors to understand key livestock market issues. Priorities included the need for more and better animal health services, for improved market coordination and for a more favourable business environment. A key issue was a taxation regime affecting around 200,000 pastoralists, resulting in them being charged each time they moved livestock back and forth between the states of Kassala and Gedarif. A livestock forum was created by 35 market stakeholders as a result of the first market mapping workshop and their first achievement was to influence the government to remove this double taxation (Griffith and Osorio, 2008).

Non-farm market based livelihoods are also important, not only for landless households, but also for farming households to diversify and reduce risk. In Nepal, training landless labourers with new skills, for example as electricians, has meant that they can find local work and no longer need to migrate to India for work for several months of the year. Enhancing the skills of blacksmiths in Nepal and Sudan to produce a range of goods in local demand has increased both their income and status within the community. It is important to ensure that new skills are connected to a viable market system which ensures sustainability of demand over time. Increasing local skills and local production contributes towards strengthening the resilience of the local economy, enhancing wealth and growth within the region. Diversifying skills and income earning opportunities increases options for people to fall back on in times of need.

Markets continue to be important during and in the aftermath of emergency situations. Inappropriate response can have a detrimental impact on market functioning which can undermine the longer term recovery of livelihoods. A set of tools and guidance notes, Emergency Market Mapping and Analysis (Albu 2010), has been designed to encourage and assist front-line humanitarian staff in sudden-onset emergencies to better understand, accommodate and make use of market-systems in the response and recovery process.

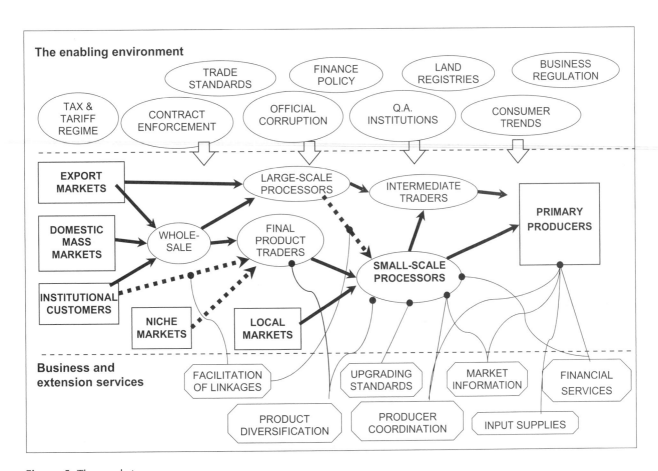

Figure 5. The market map

2.4.5 Ensuring safe living conditions

Safe living conditions refer to shelter and buildings, water supply, sanitation, safe and affordable energy and other aspects of infrastructure that people need to meet their basic needs. Living conditions are important to livelihoods and resilience as they can affect wellbeing, health and ability to work. Housing, other infrastructure and services can be affected in different ways by hazards. The assets of the most vulnerable are likely to be weakest or least protected for example homes constructed of mud and thatch are more vulnerable to storms; poorly surfaced roads to remote communities are more likely to become impassable in floods; and those dependent on drinking water from unprotected sources such as open water bodies or wells could be more vulnerable to disease or even water scarcity, as compared with managed reservoirs and protected pumps.

Why are safe living conditions important for resilience?

Safe living conditions provide people with physical comfort and security which are important contributors to wellbeing. They also contribute to human health and ability to work effectively. However, living conditions are very often adversely affected by hazards with very direct implications for human safety. Homes can be destroyed by floods, earthquakes, landslides etc resulting in physical danger, and loss of valuable belongings. Water supplies and sanitation systems can be disrupted by flooding resulting in health impacts, such as water borne disease. Roads can become blocked by landslides impacting on access to markets, schools or other service providers. To ensure that people are able to pursue secure and diverse livelihoods it is necessary to analyse all aspects of their living conditions and ensure that they are safe from the effects of hazards and stresses. After disasters occur, it is essential that recovery and reconstruction address existing vulnerabilities in living conditions through 'building back better'.

Action to ensure safe living conditions

Whilst there are many aspects of living conditions that can be vulnerable, Practical Action has particular experience of two key areas of strengthening security: housing and water supplies. In Peru

Source: Chris Martin

Building earthquake-resistant housing using quincha technology, Peru much work has been done to develop a system of construction that is resilient to earthquakes. Following a devastating earthquake in the Alto Mayo region of Peru in 1990 Practical Action became involved in a major reconstruction project to build earthquake resistant housing improving on traditional 'quincha' technology. This experience led to improvements and further application after subsequence earthquakes in 1991, 2001 and 2007. Demonstration buildings were constructed to illustrate the benefits to local people, and community groups were then engaged to participate in building their own homes and centres and to spread the technology.

Traditional quincha building uses round poles set directly in the ground; filled in with smaller wooden poles and interwoven to form a matrix, which is then plastered with one or more layers of earth. This results in a flexible structure with an inherent earthquake resistance. Improved quincha has the following characteristics over and above traditional quincha:

- Concrete foundations for greater stability and to prevent humidity affecting the wood.
- Wooden columns treated with tar or pitch to protect against humidity.
- Careful jointing between columns and beams to improve structural integrity.
- Canes woven in a vertical fashion to provide greater stability.
- Lightweight metal sheet roofing to reduce danger of falling tiles.
- Roof eaves of sufficient width to ensure protection of walls from heavy rains

In Bangladesh, Practical Action has worked with communities to develop simple and affordable flood-resistant housing and drinking water supply. These incorporate simple but effective ideas, like building the house or hand pump into a concrete plinth raised above the flood level. Constructing house walls from jute panels that cost very little yet means they are quick and easy to replace. Portable hen houses mean a family's valuable assets can be safely removed from the waters. Raising hand pumps can have a considerable impact as Moina Begum illustrates:

> Our life was very painful due to a lack of safe drinking water, particularly during floods. While the flood was ongoing we were fetching safe drinking water from one or two kilometers away. Sometimes we even used flood water to meet our needs. Every year we suffered waterborne diseases like dysentery and diarrhoea. Now we have an elevated tube well near my house. This tube well did not go under flood water in 2008.

The height of the raised plinth for flood resistant housing and hand pumps aims to be above the typical flood level. However, as climate change is bringing about more severe weather events, this level is likely to become higher in the future. This raises the importance of taking climate change, and other long term trends, into account to inform livelihood decisions (see **Section 2.5**).

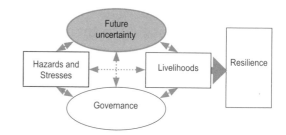

2.5 FUTURE UNCERTAINTY

A challenge faced by vulnerable communities relates to the uncertainties about their future, brought about by ever increasing changes in their natural, political, social and economic environment, many of which are beyond their control. Long term trends, such as the AIDS pandemic, population growth, civil conflicts, environmental degradation, economic globalization and rapid urbanization, are part of a dynamic context which poor people have to contend with in developing their livelihoods, and in managing hazards and stresses. The most critical current trend to impact on populations globally, but with most negative effect on the poor, is climate change (see also **Issues Page 2**). Long term trends are not the same as hazards and stresses – but they are very often an underlying causal factor (see also **Section 2.6.4**). For example, globalization is not a hazard in itself, but increasing global trade can bring commodity prices down resulting in reduced income for producer households. Some trends are outside the control of local communities whilst others, such as environmental degradation, will be influenced by both external and local factors.

What do we mean by future uncertainty?

Long term trends can have unpredictable impacts on the natural, physical, social, technological and economic environment. This in turn contributes to uncertainty about the future viability of livelihoods under new conditions, and around the predictability of certain hazards and stresses, as illustrated in the following examples:

- **Environmental degradation** contributes to vulnerability as a result of the declining productivity and value of natural assets, as well as increasing instability in the environment with the associated risks of hazards. For example, deforestation increases the risk of droughts, forest fires and desertification in arid and semi-arid areas. It also contributes to soil erosion, and slopes can become susceptible to collapse.
- **Intensification of agriculture and a decline in biodiversity** are trends that can increase the risks of food insecurity. The Green Revolution during the 1980s introduced new farming techniques including high yielding seed varieties, inorganic fertilizer, chemical pesticides and herbicides, and improved irrigation. Whilst these resulted in short term increases in output, more recent experience is showing trends of declining soil quality, resistance to pesticides and herbicides, a dramatic loss of agro-biodiversity, and depletion of ground water. Intensive production is proving to be unsustainable in the long term as compared to more agro-ecological approaches.
- **Globalization** means that decisions or policies in one country can have impacts on livelihoods in many other countries which are beyond their control. For example, bio fuels policies and commodity speculation around food crops in developed countries contributed to food price hikes in many poor countries in 2007 and 2008.
- **Migration** has resulted in increased remittances to rural communities with positive economic benefits, though it also divides families, creating potential social vulnerabilities for women and children left behind.
- **Climate change** may lead to a wide range of different future scenarios in different geographical contexts. Predictions are highly generalized and specific forecasts remain uncertain. It has been suggested that with a two degree rise in temperatures, tea growing may no longer be possible in the Kenyan highlands. It is not clear, however, what may be better suited to that environment.

Not all trends have negative implications: some can be positive. The increasing availability of information communications technologies such as the internet and mobile phones are proving to be beneficial for the rural poor. Our interest is to help equip communities to respond effectively to negative trends, but also to take advantage of positive trends.

Why is it important to recognize future uncertainty? Long term trends and climate change

In order to deal effectively with the possible outcomes of future trends, households and communities need to be able to better understand those trends and to adapt their lives and livelihoods in response to them. Whereas coping capacity relates to an ability to cope with threats or stresses in the short term, adaptive capacity is key to effectively responding to dynamic change over the long term (see **Section 2.2**).

Adaptive capacity refers to **the combination of skills, assets, networks and institutions and policies that enable communities to continually assess their own situation against the current and emerging context and make appropriate changes to their lives and livelihoods**. Recognition of the relevance of long term trends is essential if adaptive capacity is to be built. Strengthened livelihoods and preparedness for hazards and stresses can strengthen resilience in the *present*, or within a known context, but additional elements are needed to ensure resilience *over time*:

- Raising awareness and recognition of trends and their local impacts.
- Access to relevant and timely information relating to impacts and how to adapt to them.
- Confidence and flexibility to learn and experiment in order to adapt.

These three elements should not be considered independently of the other elements of the V2R framework. Diversified livelihoods, disaster preparedness and a supportive governance environment are also essential to building capacity to adapt to future uncertainty. Diversified livelihood assets and skills facilitate people's ability to explore and pursue alternative strategies as existing ones become unviable. Disaster preparedness ensures that they can cope with new or more frequent hazards and stresses associated with trends. The governance environment will need to respond to new needs resulting from trends and their impacts.

Case Study 3: Changing climate in Nepal

In Chitwan District in Nepal, Practical Action worked with the community of Kabilash between 2004 and 2007 to better understand how they are being affected by climate change. Almost all of those consulted noted changing climatic conditions in the area, particularly increasing drought and unusual rainfall patterns, including rainstorms decreasing in number but increasing in intensity. Data from the nearest two meteorological stations confirm that average precipitation has increased by 614mm and average temperature has increased by 1.3C° over the past 30 years. More than 80 per cent of the total precipitation is received in the three months between the second week of June and the first week of September.

Interviews, discussions and observations identified landslides, flash floods, unusual rainfall patterns, seasonal storms (dry winds, hail and thunder) and droughts as major hazards increasing in recent years. People have begun to observe long lasting winter fog which had not previously been seen. Higher temperatures in the daytime, particularly during summer, affects work in the fields. The frequency and magnitude of flood related disasters has also increased over the past decades.

These hazards have significant impacts on the livelihoods of the communities and the ecosystem. Erratic rainfall has multiple adverse impacts. Heavier rainfall over a shorter period prevents the proper recharge of watersheds and the available precipitation is lost through run-off and overland flow. This in turn creates landslides and flash floods, erodes fertile soil thereby decreasing productivity and ultimately degrades or destroys livelihood assets. This erratic rainfall creates seasonal scarcity of water for irrigation during the non-monsoon season, while long gaps between the two successive rains (even during the rainy season) can lead to increased frequency of droughts. Moreover, erratic rainfall prevents timely planting, care and harvesting of crops and thus decreases food production. Traditionally farmers have maintained a calendar of cropping and harvesting based on the rains and seasons, but now this calendar does not fit recent weather patterns.

Dry wind storms used to come during the pre-monsoon season between March and June, but people reported that they can now occur at any time of the year. Dry storms often destroy the roofs of houses and cattle sheds, damage crops and injure people. Hail storms have also become common but unpredictable events in recent years. They destroy crops and corrugated zinc roofs, kill wild birds and destroy their nests and eggs, which results in an increase in insect pests in crops.

Source: Ensor J. and R. Berger (2009) *Understanding Climate Change Adaptation*, pp. 58–59, Practical Action Publishing, Rugby, UK.

Measures to protect drinking water pipes during floods in Nepal

Source: Practical Action

Issues Page 2. Climate Change

Climate change is defined as a change in the climate that persists for decades or longer, arising from human activity. It is now widely accepted that the global climate is changing, principally as a result of burning fossil fuels which in turn contribute to a greenhouse effect. According to the United Nations Intergovernmental Panel on Climate Change (IPCC) 4th Assessment Report in 2007, the average temperature of the earth's surface is expected to increase by about three degrees centigrade, on average, over the next century, assuming greenhouse gas emissions continue to rise at current rates. This temperature rise is causing changing rainfall patterns, rising sea levels, and more unpredictable weather events.

Climate change impacts

The impacts of climate change are complex and uncertain, but principally they fall into two categories. Firstly, there will be more frequent, more extreme and more unpredictable occurrences of discrete recurring hazards, such as floods, droughts, hurricanes, cyclones, and so on. Impacts of these hazards include more frequent or extensive loss of harvest and more frequent or extensive damage to homes and infrastructure.

Secondly, new stresses will emerge, such as gradual increases in temperature or decreases in rainfall, or changes in seasonal patterns – for example the timing of monsoon rains can in turn have a number of different impacts including the gradual reduction of harvests due to changes in land, soil and water quality and quantity and the emergence of new hazards (new types of pest outbreak or disease for example).

These impacts are being felt disproportionately by the poor. Firstly, because the impacts of climate change are occurring more quickly in sub equatorial regions where most poor people live. Secondly, most are rural producers reliant on natural resources and regular weather patterns (for example rainfall) for their production. Gradual changes in the climate and natural environment are putting disproportionate pressures on their livelihoods. Furthermore, hazard coping strategies suited to normal climate variability are no longer adequate under increasing variability from climate change.

Climate change and uncertainty

Climate change contributes to vulnerability by creating greater uncertainty in the environment within which poor people are living and producing, for example it is making previously relatively predictable weather patterns more unpredictable. For the majority of weather-related hazards and stresses communities have built up considerable knowledge about their characteristics based on historical experience (for example timing of monsoon rains, patterns of cyclones, seasons of heavy frost probability), but increasing climate variability is causing them to be much more difficult to predict, perceive and measure.

At a global level climate change predictions vary hugely depending on assumptions about trends in future industrialization and consumption patterns (increasing greenhouse gas emissions) as opposed to more optimistic assumptions about the emergence of cleaner technologies and stronger policy lines on emission reduction (carbon dioxide stabilization). Predictions of impacts at the national and local level are extremely challenging, due to the range of factors and feedback loops that could affect future climate, and the lack of capacity to gather and analyse data for all regions.

Climate change adaptation

Where reliable information about the future is available, communities can be assisted to prepare for and adapt to those changes, for example where it is predicted that rainfall will diminish, more drought tolerant crops, rainwater harvesting technologies, and improved crop storage may help. However, where predictions are less reliable adaptive capacity should be strengthened – ensuring that communities are able to access a range of skills, resources and information that they can draw on in order to continuously shape their livelihoods as the environment changes around them.

Adaptive strategies should be desirable, rather than the only available option, pursued out of desperation. In other words, such strategies should emerge as a positive result of an assessment of relevant information, and consideration of different options available through employing assets and skills in new ways. In the Andean region of Ancash, Peru (see **Case Study 2, above**), the effects of climate change have led to more frequent crop losses from heavy frosts. The main coping strategy has been for some or all family members to migrate to the town in search of waged employment resulting in de-population and decline of the community. More desirable adaptive strategies for the community which are being explored are to improve and extend livestock production which is less adversely affected by the weather and to rebuild biodiversity amongst their potato crop, reviving frost and drought resistant varieties.

Action at the community level is known as Community Based Adaptation. There is significant evidence that programmes at the local level can achieve much in terms of increasing the resilience and adaptive capacity of communities to cope with climate change. However, complementary action is necessary at other levels to support and facilitate community based adaptation, to make the necessary funds available, and to reduce further emissions at a global level (see **Section 2.6**).

Finally, it is worth noting that work to help communities to adapt to a changing climate are based on an assumption that action will be taken at an international level to ensure that global temperatures do not increase by more than two degrees centigrade above pre industrial levels. If this stabilization is not achieved, and temperatures rise by four degrees or more then there will be vastly increased risks to livelihoods and ecosystems and more radical strategies will need to be considered.

Source: Practical Action

Sharon Loorameta, a Maasai Project Officer for Practical Action, speaks at LiveEarth in 2007

2.5.1 Raising awareness and recognizing trends and their local impacts

Many long term trends which contribute to uncertainty can be complex, and can originate from sources distant from where they have most impact. For these reasons they are often not readily recognized or understood at the local level. The long term implications of inorganic fertilizer application in terms of loss of soil structure and important minerals may not be perceived or easily grasped by farmers with no formal education. The impacts of climate change at the local level are often incomprehensible to communities who are accustomed to a reliable climate, and have no understanding of the complex global processes which are contributing to localized changes in weather patterns.

Why is raising awareness and recognizing trends and their local impacts important?

A clearer recognition of trends and their local impacts is important in order for individuals and communities to act on this knowledge when those trends are likely to make their livelihoods unviable. Adaptation should ideally be proactive assessment of options, rather than a purely reactive response to change. Lack of understanding of trends can lead to inappropriate planning, for example failure to adapt based on an assumption that changing weather patterns will return to normal. Awareness raising of relevant trends is therefore an important activity at the community level to ensure that they are taken into account in hazard and livelihood analysis (see **Section 3.2**) to inform future planning (see **Section 3.3**).

Raising awareness of the local impacts of negative trends amongst other stakeholder groups at other levels (district, national, international) can also be important to strengthen the impetus for mitigation of those trends where possible or relevant. The trend towards privatisation of extension services results in a service gap to the poor, who are rarely reached by private agro-dealer services. Raising awareness of this gap can encourage the adaptation of privatised service models, or the maintenance of some public or subsidised services, to ensure that the needs of the poor are better met. Increasing the recognition of the impacts of climate change on the poor can add to the imperative in the global north to reduce greenhouse gas emissions.

Action to improve awareness and recognition of trends and their local impacts

Improving recognition of trends and their impacts can be achieved through awareness raising and educational activities. In the case of climate change, Practical Action has supported awareness raising activities, through schools, directly with communities, through various types of media (radio, television) and via other institutions, such as research programmes. In Ancash, Peru, youth theatre and radio were used as media for communicating messages about climate change: its causes and potential consequences.

Practical Action has also supported documentation and communication of the negative impacts of some long term trends on the poor, in order to influence policy and practice. Research in Tharaka, Kenya, during the 1990s, aimed to better understand the trend of biodiversity loss, and the impact this was having on the resilience of food production over time. This research fed into a process of advocacy for an international seed treaty that would ensure that the germplasm that underlies the biodiversity of major food crops was not captured by private interests. It was also used to promote the importance of including agricultural diversity in the Convention on Biological Diversity.

Similarly, local impacts of climate change are being gathered and shared with decision-makers and the general public. Practical Action staff have used their knowledge of communities struggling to adapt to climate change to influence international climate negotiators at the four last annual Conference of the Parties (COP) meetings of the United Nations Framework Convention on Climate Change (UNFCCC). Shortly after the COP12 held in Nairobi, Kenya in 2007, a member of Practical Action's East Africa office was invited to speak on behalf of Massai communities affected by climate change at the Live Earth concert in London, UK, which was broadcast around the world.

2.5.2 Ensuring access to relevant and timely information

An awareness of trends is important. However, in addition, access to relevant and timely information about the nature and frequency of their impacts and how to respond or adapt to them, is essential if communities are to be able to effectively respond and adapt. Such information might include the following:

Table 5. Trends, impacts and adaptation options	
Information about trends and impacts • climate science, long range climate predictions and short range forecasts; • implications of policy trends, for example what would the privatisation of intellectual property such as germplasm mean for farming communities; • implications of processes such as desertification for crop production.	**Information about adaptation options** • access to, and management of, traditional and new seed varieties; • skills in managing emerging livestock pests and diseases; • improved soil and water conservation strategies to help cope with drought; • skills to pursue entirely new, possibly non-farm, livelihood options.

The flow of information needs to be two-way – not only a delivery of relevant information to communities about trends and adaptation options but also a flow from communities to decision makers, researchers, and other service providers to improve their understanding of the local context, priorities and needs.

Why is access to relevant and timely information important for building resilience?

Information is important in order to inform decision making and action at the community and household level. This includes both information about the nature and impact of trends, as well as information about adaptation options. For example, if an impact of climate change is increased salinity of groundwater, those with good links to research and extension agencies can find out more about the implications of this trend and can access inputs such as salt tolerant varieties of rice in order to adapt their livelihoods.

Information about long term trends is often complex as the outcomes of such processes are not always predictable, and may vary according to local context. In terms of climate change, much attention is paid to accessing mid and long range climate forecasts in order to inform adaptation strategies. However, such information is still highly generalized and uncertain. In such cases it is more relevant to ensure access to a wide range of options for adaptation to different climate outcomes.

Action to improve access to relevant and timely information

Practical Action strengthens communities' access to relevant information on an ongoing basis through strengthening networks and linkages with other institutions. These might include research institutes, meteorological offices, weather stations, service providers, and other governmental and non-governmental agencies. The stronger the knowledge networks that communities have, the better able they are to access information, ideas and resources to aid adaptation. Such networks should facilitate a two-way flow, so that information also flows upwards to actors in the governance environment (see **Section 2.6**) to improve their understanding of the local context and needs. This in turn helps to ensure that they are able to respond in an appropriate way, i.e. to communicate relevant information in easily accessible styles, formats, media and language.

In Frias, a northern valley in Peru, farming communities have found that weather patterns are changing and traditional indicators of weather patterns (such as bird migrations, plant flowerings) are no longer accurate. They were also unable to access information about climate trends at the local level. In collaboration with a local university, they have thus been collecting this data themselves. Rainfall and temperature are monitored in a number of households at different elevations of the valley. This is shared with researchers who interpret the information and share findings back to the community. The information is also being fed up to the state meteorological offices. Researchers are also supporting communities in accessing information about which new crops are suited at different elevations, and how to address new pest and disease outbreaks, as the climate changes. Some farmers are already making changes to their crop selection in response to impacts they are experiencing.

Community extension services are critical in order to facilitate access to up to date information, skills and technologies that will be relevant to adapting to various long term trends. As noted in **Section 2.4.3**, they form an essential link between communities and researchers and other services providers. The challenge now is to ensure that community extension agents themselves are aware of the necessity for a dynamic approach to assessing needs amongst their clients, and enhancing their ability to continually update knowledge to respond to a changing context.

2.5.3 Building confidence and flexibility to learn and experiment

Adaptation requires skills in thinking through possible scenarios for an uncertain future, and confidence to experiment with alternative livelihoods activities, such as new crops, and innovate with new technologies, such as alternative water management strategies. This requires new capacities and confidence to continue to innovate and take calculated risks based on regular processes of reflection and learning. Just as strong networks (horizontal and vertical) are important for accessing information, they are also relevant to supporting the exchange of practical experiences.

Why is building confidence and flexibility to learn and experiment important?

Clearly planning and decision making is more challenging under uncertain conditions. Livelihoods strategies and technologies that work in the present may not function as environmental factors change over time. Many households and communities facing uncertainties caused by long term trends, particularly climate change, struggle to envisage how they can build their future and continue to move out of poverty. Some may feel forced to leave their communities and find alternative livelihoods in urban centres. Others feel disempowered, anxious and unconfident about the future.

Alongside processes to support awareness and recognition of long term trends, and access to relevant and timely information, confidence and flexibility are needed in order for households and communities to be able to explore new pathways and adapt to change. Confidence and flexibility can be strengthened in two key ways: developing technological capabilities, and strengthening horizontal (as well as vertical) networks of support and exchange of experience. Building technology capabilities have been described briefly in **Issues Page 1: Technology for Resilient Communities**. This is about enabling resource poor women and men to identify and develop technologies to address their needs as these needs change over time. Rather than simply helping people to access and use new technologies, it involves improving their ability to assess, develop and adapt technologies – both new and traditional – in a changing environment. It may involve reviving traditional practices and adapting them to new circumstances or seeking new ideas from other sources, but adapting them to the local context.

The importance of vertical networks was outlined in the previous section, improving the flow of information, including skills and technologies, between communities and others within the governance environment. Horizontal networks between households, communities and civil society groups are also important to facilitate the sharing of practical experiences with coping with change. Community extension workers can play an important role in facilitating local learning, alongside other communications tools, and exchange visits.

Action to build confidence and flexibility to learn and experiment

Trends of temperature increases and sea level rise, combined with failing irrigation systems, are contributing to increased salinity in the rice paddy fields of small scale farmers in Sri Lanka. Work by Practical Action raised awareness of climate change as a potential cause, helped farmers to access relevant information and seed resources, and, critically, supported them to carry out variety selection research. Following poor experience with fertilizer-dependent hybrid varieties, the capacity and confidence to experiment with indigenous varieties was revived and farmers developed qualitative indicators for selection and scored varieties according to their own preferences. These experiences and skills were then shared with farmers in other saline areas through learning networks. Ongoing relationships were also fostered with a national seed organization and the nearby rice research institute.

In Ancash, Peru, Practical Action has initiated a School of Resilient Farmer Leaders, through which local resource people are trained in various aspects of improved production. As climate change is already having a significant impact on local livelihoods, farmers must also be able to adapt their farming practices over time to cope with continuing changes in climate. Not only do trained farmer leaders transfer the new ideas and technologies to their communities, but each household adopting a new technology is encouraged to pass on knowledge to others through a revolving system. Improved guinea pig breeds have been introduced to cross with local varieties leading to increased reproductive rate and animal size, without losing the characteristics of resistance to the cold climate. As the nucleus breeding stock is transferred from household to household, lessons are shared and confidence is strengthened.

Source: Katherine Pasteur, Practical Action

Improved guinea pig production, Ancash, Peru

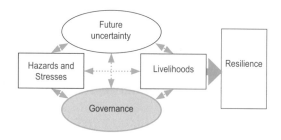

2.6 GOVERNANCE

People's vulnerability is shaped by a whole range of public and private organizations, institutions, policies and legislation that affect their lives. These structures operate at all levels from the household and local community through to the international level. They include not just formal organizations and laws but also informal structures such as cultural codes of conduct. The governance context refers to the range or different formal and informal organizations, policies and practices operating at different levels from local to international.

Government, NGOs and the private sector all have roles to play in strengthening people's livelihoods and in providing support to communities to prepare for and respond to hazards and stresses. However, such institutions frequently fail to provide services and policies which meet the needs of the most vulnerable communities or sectors of the population. Prevailing power structures, economic systems, cultural factors and political ideologies can all underlie these governance issues.

What do we mean by governance?

The term governance embraces a whole range of public and private, formal and informal organizations, policies, and processes, operating at local, national and international levels, which impact on different aspects of livelihoods, disaster preparedness or capacity to adapt to future uncertainty. Table 6 gives some examples.

Table 6. Examples of governance factors		
Organizations		
Public	Agricultural extension departments	Access to information for livelihoods and adaptation to climate change
	Civil protection structures	Effective support to disaster preparedness
Private	Savings and credit organizations	Ability of poor people to access credit to invest in livelihoods or save for times of need
Civil society	Farmers Unions	Representation of farmer needs in policy fora
	Climate lobbying organizations	Communicating how climate change impacts disproportionately on the poor
Policies and processes		
Policy	National land-use policies	Access to land for livelihoods. Land use planning to reduce hazard exposure.
	International trade policy	Cheap imports undermine local production
Legislation	Construction standards	Safety and hazard resistance of infrastructure
	General rule of law	Security of people and their property
Institutions	Power relations in communities	Access to land, water and other resources for livelihoods
	Gender relations in households	Responsibilities for disaster response

Institutional analysis is an essential process for understanding the roles and agendas of these different organizations, policies and processes (see **Case Study 4**). There are very often differences between policy on paper and what happens in practice which need to be explored. Informal institutions (for example see **Issues Page 3: Gender**) can have a powerful influence over the vulnerability of certain groups in society. Institutional analysis should appraise the opportunities and constraints presented by the governance environment and identify areas for action.

Why is the governance context important for building resilience?

Consideration of the governance context is vital to building resilience, because it determines how people can access resources, skills, technologies and markets to strengthen and diversify their livelihoods, how they protect themselves from hazards, and how they access support to help them recover when they are affected. The institutional and policy context can act as an enabling environment, making it easier for people to improve their livelihoods, reduce their exposure to hazards, and adapt to climate change. However, the most vulnerable are typically poorly organized and lack voice in decision-making process that might affect them. They often lack access to the kinds of services which could help them to improve their livelihoods or to prepare for or respond to shocks and stresses.

Service providers, in turn, are often not oriented towards the poor. Their training prepares them for dealing with better-off sectors of society, with whom they more easily relate. They are usually located in urban centres some distance from poor and marginal communities. Understanding the needs of the poor, and finding more participatory ways to consult with and involve them in decision-making can be a cultural and a practical challenge. Weak linkages between local level practicalities and national level decision making further exacerbates the challenges. Messages from the local level are not adequately fed up to national policy makers. The influence of other actors, such as big business or other vested interests, can on the other hand, be strong leading to policy outcomes that are inappropriate, or even bad for the poor.

Action relating to the governance context

Addressing governance issues at various levels is essential to complement any work in communities, if impacts are to be sustained and long term change is to be achieved at scale. An enabling environment is necessary to replicate the examples of success outlined in earlier chapters. This type of work is inevitably complex and challenging, and impacts cannot be guaranteed within relatively short project timeframes. However, it must not be sidelined.

Work to effectively address the governance context aims to enhance the voice of communities and the responsiveness of relevant institutions and policy. It tends to fall under the following headings:

- advocating for decentralized and participatory decision making;
- strengthening links between local, district and national levels;
- promoting integrated approaches to livelihoods, disasters and climate change;
- addressing underlying systemic issues.

Case Study 4: Institutional analysis of drought in Zimbabwe

An institutional analysis of drought was carried out in 2009 in order to understand the historical and institutional dynamics of drought risk reduction and management in Bulilima and Mangwe districts in Zimbabwe. Findings from focus group discussions and timelines/trend analysis revealed that there were four major droughts between 1980 and 2000 in the years 1982-4 and the devastating drought of 1991/92.

The government was actively involved during periods of emergency and provided grain through loan schemes administered through the Department of Social Welfare. The government also assisted households with school fees during droughts. Several NGOs offered relief services to communities, for example the Catholic Development Commission provided food relief and ran a food for work programme. However, farmers were not always happy with NGO response targeting policies, for example using selective targeting based on livestock asset ownership. Households prefer block targeting for humanitarian interventions.

In terms of drought risk reduction, farmers see government departments as having weak capacity to deliver appropriate services. They point out that agricultural extension outreach is poor due to lack of resources, though in cases where extension workers get to the communities, the training and knowledge dissemination is good. Farmers were not happy with the Department of Veterinary Services (DVS) which reportedly distributes drugs late when there is a disease outbreak. Grain marketing policies were found not to favour crops that do well in the district. There is heavy emphasis on maize production, which does not tolerate the semi-arid conditions of the district.

Some NGOs give technical assistance and financial/material support for initiatives that help communities in rebuilding their livelihoods. The institutional analysis revealed that NGO coordination is limited because they do want to work in the same geographical areas, and there are conflicts over beneficiaries.

Finally, the study observed a failure of agricultural policy to address the new context of climate change. Climate change has resulted in declining crop yields, water availability, increased crop and livestock diseases and increased dry spells. However, there is no evidence of policies that have a focus on water harvesting, nor marketing bias towards drought tolerant crops.

Source: Sithembisiwe Mpofu (2009) 'Coping With Drought: Drought Coping Strategies in Matebeleland South', unpublished report, Practical Action.

Source: Practical Action

Drought in Zimbabwe is leading to devastating impacts

Issues Page 3. Gender

An important informal institution is gender – the different roles, behaviours and activities of men and women that have been deemed appropriate by a particular society. Women's position is society often makes them more vulnerable than men. They tend to have less access to livelihood resources and income earning opportunities. Women tend to be under-represented in decision-making processes due to various factors including active exclusion by men, lack of time to participate due to domestic responsibilities, and lack of confidence to express their views. At the same time they bear a heavy social and economic burden: taking responsibility for domestic tasks such as producing and cooking food, fetching water, looking after children and caring for the sick and elderly.

When hazards occur, women play important roles in ensuring the safety of younger or older members of the family. However, social factors may make them reluctant to move from their home to a safer area, or they may be less aware than men of how to respond. Women's physical size, strength and endurance tend to be less than that of men, and in an emergency they may be slowed down by children. Despite these challenges, experience has shown that women have extraordinary strengths and determination under challenging circumstances, and often play a proactive role in the restoration of household and community functions when hazards and stresses occur.

Gender analysis and empowerment

Gender analysis is the study of the different roles of women and men to understand what they do, what resources they have and what their needs and priorities are. During a V2R analysis it is important to talk to women and men separately in order to understand the particular challenges they face, as well as their strengths and the opportunities for empowerment. Actions very often need to be tailored to ensure that women are able to participate equally, for example training courses should be held at times of day when women are able to attend. Providing child care can improve attendance. Training may need to be tailored to the educational level of women. Raising awareness of the risks and the transmission of early warning messages may also need gender consideration. Formal dissemination through written material, broadcasts or public meetings may not reach women who tend to acquire information through more informal means.

A key challenge is ensuring that the deep-rooted social inequalities between men and women are addressed and that women's voices continue to be represented in decision-making over the long term. Disasters, in upsetting social norms, often create a space for challenging inequality and pushing for women's empowerment, but there may be backlashes against women who begin to speak out and challenge social structures, for example in the form of domestic violence. It is therefore important to view addressing gender disparities as a long term process, rather than a one-off project activity. Addressing gender issues must also be a multi-level process, so that gender perspectives are incorporated into formal policies and institutions relating to disasters and livelihoods from local to national levels.

2.6.1 Ensuring decentralized and participatory decision-making

Often the needs of the poor are not taken into account in decision-making and adequate services do not reach them in remote and vulnerable areas. When they are not well-organized the poor lack the capacity to access and influence relevant decision-making processes, and those in authority frequently do not create space for the poor to participate. National-level policy or legislative decisions are often poorly enforced at the local level, or necessary resources are not decentralized to implement them. It is important to ensure that governance structures are oriented to facilitate access by and participation of poor and marginalized populations.

Why is ensuring decentralized and participatory decision making important?

Many rural communities are more vulnerable because they are unable to access services, such as water provision, agricultural extension, health and education. Public sector workers (school teachers, health workers, or extension providers) often fail to fully attend to their duties in vulnerable communities because they lack resources and motivation to reach often remote locations. Government extension services and private input suppliers are also often unaware of the specific challenges faced by poor, remote and vulnerable producers. Their training has tended to educate them to serve better-off farmers who can afford and access external inputs, which may be neither appropriate nor available to those who are isolated from market linkages.

The failure to implement or enforce national level regulations and standards (such as environmental assessment procedures, or land use planning guidelines) at district level is often responsible for exacerbating the occurrence of hazards, or creating vulnerable livelihood conditions. For example disease outbreaks in urban slums are frequently the result of a lack of enforcement of sanitary planning regulations which might have reduced such widespread exposure. Power, knowledge and resources are needed at the meso (district) level, so that local government and other front line institutions and service providers can consult with and respond to communities and meet their specific needs. In part this is a matter of policy, to ensure that power and resources are decentralized. However, it is also an issue of education and attitudes, for staff at this level to have the skills and motivation to listen and respond to community groups and other representatives of the poor.

Action to ensure decentralized and participatory decision making

Practical Action works to strengthen capacity at the district level to implement policy and to facilitate community level processes. In Nepal, Practical Action has built the capacity of government and other local NGO staff to facilitate community vulnerability analysis so that district development budget decisions can be formulated in response to the identified priorities. In Sudan, local government administrative officers have been trained in Participatory Action Plan Development, a process for planning in natural resource allocation and use and resolving associated conflicts. In the rainforest belt of Peru, where Andean communities are migrating into areas occupied by the native Awajun, Practical Action has built the capacity of the Awajun Federation to negotiate over land issues with incoming settlers, engaging all stakeholders in regional government including the judiciary.

In Peru, excellent national policy exists for decentralized and participatory budgeting, with structures and mechanisms for municipal level allocation of budgets. However, in practice finances do not tend to be accessed by communities to meet pressing livelihood and disaster related needs. This is due in part to a lack of capacity at the community level to submit the necessary applications for funds, and in part to a lack of understanding by municipal government of the kinds of needs and constraints faced by communities. Practical Action has worked with communities in the municipalities of Yungay and Huaraz to help them to produce their own local development plans, which they submitted to the participatory budget process. At the same time, Practical Action staff liaised with municipal staff to raise their awareness of the practical needs of rural communities, relating to livelihoods, disasters and climate change, such that they have become more supportive of their applications.

2.6.2 Strengthening links between local, national and international levels

For national and international institutions and policies to be oriented towards the context and needs of vulnerable communities, there needs to be effective communication from the grassroots upwards. Equally, national and international policy and plans must be fed down to regional, district and local levels to ensure that they are implemented effectively or to allow communities to respond when they are deemed inappropriate. These processes require strong linkages between the various structures and organizations operating at different levels.

Why is strengthening the links between local, national and international levels important?

All too often there are huge gaps between policy and institutional rhetoric at the national level and community needs at the local level. This can easily result in wasted resources on the part of institutions, and frustration and continuing vulnerability for poor communities. Policies that contribute to building the resilience of the poor need to be based on a good understanding of the people's livelihoods and the risks and trends they face, the reality of service provision at local levels, and the kinds of interventions that have proved successful in bringing about change. Best practice by NGOs, local government and others working at the local level must be well linked into wider organizational structures, and must also seek to influence policy where it is not helpful, if they are not to remain isolated examples of excellence. This also holds true for international policies, decisions and processes, for example to change those which contribute to negative trends such as climate change, economic instability, and low prices for small producers.

Action to strengthen links between local, district and national levels

Links can be strengthened informing and influencing organizations and policies at different levels, or establishing processes or structures which facilitate knowledge sharing, from the bottom up and from the top down (see Practical Action's working model for achieving impact at scale, **Section 4.1.4**). In Peru, Practical Action has worked through the Round Table on Poverty Reduction to strengthen the integration of disaster risk reduction into development planning. Practical Action's grassroots experience has fed into the production, together with the National Round Table, of a practical manual on integrating Disaster Risk Reduction (DRR) into local planning. This network is now sharing the manual with 700 affiliated local governments, and Practical Action aims to provide capacity building to support its uptake. The influential Round Table is also lobbying at the national level for policy change to ensure 10 per cent of participatory budget allocations at municipal level are allocated to DRR activities.

Grassroots monitoring of national or international policy implementation is another strategy for ensuring that commitments are translated into action. At an international level the Hyogo Framework for Action (HFA) is a global blueprint for disaster risk reduction efforts during the next decade. Its goal is to substantially reduce disaster losses by 2015 – in lives, and in the social, economic, and environmental assets of communities and countries. The framework sets out responsibilities, priorities for action, and practical means for achieving disaster resilience for vulnerable communities, for those states and for international organizations. Governments of 168 countries have signed up to ensuring that disaster risk reduction is a national and a local priority with a strong institutional basis for implementation. In many countries action was slow to follow, and so the Global Network for Civil Society Organizations for DRR initiated a process of grassroots monitoring of implementation of the Hyogo framework, publishing its findings to encourage further action (2009).

Practical Action has also proposed and promoted a national governance structure that would facilitate links between international, national and local levels for the funding and implementation of Community Based Adaptation (CBA). This would involve national stakeholder forums which would receive funding and regional or international technical support and coordinate adaptation planning and equitable resource distribution at the local level. The forum would facilitate representation and accountability for civil society organizations and local / district government with the roles of planning, implementing and monitoring CBA (Ensor and Burger 2009).

2.6.3 Promoting integrated approaches to livelihoods, disasters and climate change

The introduction to this document outlined the distinct livelihoods, disasters and climate change perspectives and the rationale for greater integration. This is relevant not only in the context of NGO interventions to support communities, but for all organizations working to strengthen community and household resilience, including government. Government departments addressing rural or agricultural development, disaster response and climate change tend to work in isolation from one another, often within different Ministries. Efforts to bring their thinking closer together can reap important rewards in terms of reducing duplication and improving effectiveness on the ground.

Why is promoting integrated approaches important for building resilience?

Disaster management policies are formulated at a national level in most countries, as are development policies. These guide the practices of institutions at various levels from the national to the district level. Disaster management policies tend to focus on preparedness and response to major natural and technological disasters. Similarly, newly evolving climate related policies frequently relate to infrastructure to protect against more extreme hazards. Neither pay sufficient attention to reducing vulnerability or strengthening livelihoods. Furthermore, implementation of development, disaster and climate related policies tend to be separate, under the control of different Ministries, with the result that they are poorly integrated in local level planning and practice. This can lead to disjointed activities at the community level and wasted time and resources.

Communities do not view disasters, development and climate change as separate issues to be analysed and addressed through different processes at different times. They are all integral to their lives and ability to make a livelihood and improve their wellbeing, and should be tackled in an integrated way. Increasingly NGOs are realizing the benefits of integrating their work, and are developing frameworks, tools and organization structures to help facilitate this. However, other institutions, including governments, have a long way to go. Much can be done to raise awareness of the benefits of integration, and strategies for moving in that direction.

Action to promote integrated approaches

Practical Action has done much to promote the integration of livelihoods thinking into sections of government responsible for disaster management and rural development through its DFID funded Livelihood Centred Approaches to Disaster Risk Reduction Project (2006-2010). Building capacity for participatory vulnerability analysis and action planning for building resilience has been a useful strategy for engaging different stakeholders at village and district level in understanding the different factors that contribute towards vulnerability and how resilience can be strengthened. This has helped in raising their awareness of the challenges and needs of vulnerable communities, and in orienting services and projects in order to better respond. In Nepal, Bangladesh and Zimbabwe, district government capacity has been built to support integrated analysis and planning in communities, and the outcomes of those plans have then been incorporated into district or sub-district development plans. In Ancash, Peru, as a result of awareness-raising, communities are now represented in the district participatory budgeting process, and funds have been allocated to integrated projects in three rural communities.

In Sri Lanka, the Disaster Management Act of 2005 established the Disaster Management Centre, responsible for disaster mitigation, prevention and response. Practical Action has a Memorandum of Understanding with the centre to provide technical support including promoting a livelihood centred approach to disaster management. Their advice has led to the establishment of an integrated Provincial Disaster Management Committee responsible for coordinating development planning incorporating livelihoods, housing, roads and infrastructure to ensure hazard risk and mitigation measures are included. They have also delivered training to build the capacity of government officials to implement integrated disaster management and development plans.

Whilst the project described above principally focused on integrating disaster and development approaches, it has also incorporated elements which support people in dealing with the uncertainties caused by climate change. Although this was not in the project outline at the outset, given the realities within communities, addressing this issue has been unavoidable. Within the UK, Practical Action organized a high profile event for other NGOs, academics and policy makers to facilitate sharing of practical field experiences, institutional changes and implementation frameworks relating to integration of their work on livelihoods, disasters and climate change adaptation. The popularity of the event reflected the widespread interest in this issue, and the discussions and action around this theme are continuing.

2.6.4 Addressing underlying systemic issues

Underlying many of the governance issues that relate to vulnerability are more deeply rooted systemic issues which may operate at a national or global level. These include political ideologies, economic principles, geopolitical power structures, cultural factors, etc. Although these issues may seem distant from vulnerable communities, and well beyond their control, they can exert a powerful influence on the possibilities for change at all levels. Despite their systemic nature, there may be possibilities for influencing these issues through international advocacy and alliances.

Why is addressing underlying systemic issues important for building resilience?

Action at the local level may bring about change in the short term within a limited number of communities. However, in many cases the forces that drive vulnerability are related to systemic inequalities within society, within the global economy and in political structures. Therefore, without addressing these more fundamental factors, we will not bring about long term change. Conflict is often caused by ethnic or religious differences, or unequal distribution of economic resources. Livelihood opportunities are often limited by global trade regimes which make it possible for local markets to be flooded with cheap produce which undermines local production. Climate change is failing to be addressed due to geopolitical and economic factors that make it impossible for global leaders to agree to a regime to limit greenhouse gas emissions.

Systemic causes of vulnerability are diverse, highly complex, and are often deeply rooted, being based on long standing historical factors, including colonialism, or widely adopted ideologies, such as neo-liberal economics.

- Social factors include divisions in society linked to inequality, greed, prejudice (for example class, caste, creed, ethnicity, gender), values and norms, religious beliefs and understandings of rights and responsibilities.
- Economic factors include principles, trade regimes and resource distribution.
- Political factors include ideologies, priorities, patronage and colonialism.

This should not, however, detract from the importance to assessing the role of systemic issues, and seeking opportunities for action.

Action to address systemic issues

At the heart of Practical Action's strategy is a commitment to strive for social justice, equity and accountability – to tackle the systemic issues that underlie vulnerability. These deep rooted factors are principally addressed through advocacy and lobbying work at national and international levels, often through alliances with other development organizations and civil society. Working within UK coalitions such as Make Poverty History (2005-2006) and Stop Climate Chaos (2006 onward), Practical Action has played a collaborative role in raising public awareness around the need for global action to redress global economic inequality, as well as the injustice of carbon dioxide emissions by developed countries impacting first and hardest on the developing world. Both of these alliances lobbied UK government in favour of more just national and international policies and processes. They also aimed to change public understandings of these critical issues, and encourage a greater sense of personal responsibility, particularly around taking action on climate change.

Another issue on which Practical Action has lobbied hard to bring about systemic change is food justice (see **Issues Page 4: Food sovereignty**). The systemic factors that underlie insecure access to food in developing countries are complex including historical power structures and trading relationships (for example based on colonial ties); current trade regimes based on global liberalization; weak governance of an ever more powerful private sector which controls the vast majority of world food production; intellectual property rights regimes which again favour big business and disenfranchise small producers; and agricultural research and policy (national and international) which favours large scale over small scale producers. These factors have led to a situation where small scale producers are increasingly marginalized, and access to food by the poor has become ever more precarious, as demonstrated by the food shortages experienced in many countries in 2008.

Although Practical Action aims to address food security through local and national actions to improve access to resources, technologies, support services, and markets, the broader systemic factors continue to make their production marginal and their livelihoods insecure. Practical Action therefore also works at a transnational level to promote policies which address systemic inequalities. In partnership with pastoralist and farmer's leaders from East Africa, we have challenged intellectual property laws that prevent small-scale food providers and communities from developing, saving, exchanging and selling seeds, livestock breeds and fish species, and demanded the implementation of the in situ conservation and farmers' rights provisions of the FAO International Treaty on Plant Genetic Resources for Food and Agriculture and for similar global regulation of Animal Genetic Resources. We have supported the organization of seminars to emphasize to European decision makers the need to protect local food systems from food and technology dumping through changes in the Common Agriculture Policy, European Trade Policy and Competition Policy. We have worked with partners to expose decision-makers in the United Kingdom, the European Commission, and FAO to the significance of ecological agriculture for global food provision and raise awareness of food sovereignty as a small-scale food providers' alternative to the dominant food policy framework.

Source: Zul Mukida, Practical Action Sri Lanka

Ability to save and exchange seed varieties is essential to small-scale farmers

Issues Page 4. Food sovereignty

Practical Action supports the Food Sovereignty Framework as a means to challenge the dominant food production model based on industrial scale farming and liberalized, trade based global distribution. Food Sovereignty is advocated by a number of organizations of farmers, pastoralists, fisher folk and others, who aim to realize the right of peoples to define their own food, agriculture, livestock and fisheries systems. The call for Food Sovereignty was reaffirmed in Rome in November 2009, when 642 people from 93 countries, representing 450 organizations and movements of small-scale food providers, gathered at the People's Food Sovereignty Forum and committed to 'strengthen and promote our ecological model of food provision in the framework of food sovereignty that feeds all populations including those in marginal zones.'

Food Sovereignty focuses on six principles:

- Focus on food for people. Food sovereignty puts the right to sufficient, healthy and culturally appropriate food for all, at the centre of food, agriculture, livestock and fisheries policies; and rejects the proposition that food is just another commodity or component for international agri-business.
- Value food providers. Food sovereignty values and supports the contributions, and respects the rights, of women and men, peasants and small scale family farmers, pastoralists, artisanal fisher folk, forest dwellers, indigenous peoples and agricultural and fisheries workers, including migrants, who cultivate, grow, harvest and process food.
- Localize food systems. Food sovereignty puts providers and consumers at the centre of decision-making on food issues; protects food providers from the dumping of food and food aid in local markets; protects consumers from poor-quality and unhealthy food, inappropriate food aid and food tainted with genetically modified organisms.
- Put control locally. Food sovereignty places control over territory, land, grazing, water, seeds, livestock and fish populations on local food providers and respects their rights. They can use and share them in socially and environmentally sustainable ways which conserve diversity.
- Build knowledge and skills. Food sovereignty builds on the skills and local knowledge of food providers and their local organizations that conserve, develop and manage localized food production and harvesting systems, developing appropriate research systems to support this and passing on this wisdom to future generations.
- Work with nature. Food sovereignty uses the contributions of nature in diverse, low external input agro-ecological production and harvesting methods that maximize the contribution of ecosystems and improve resilience and adaptation, especially in the face of climate change.

Source: Synthesis Report, Nyéléni 2007 – Forum for Food Sovereignty, Sélingué, Mali, 23–27 February 2007, www.nyeleni2007.org

PART 3
V2R ANALYSIS AND ACTION

3.1 INTRODUCTION

This section looks at practical steps for carrying out analysis and action with communities and other stakeholders to help them move from vulnerability to resilience. Many practitioners will be familiar with existing tools for Vulnerability and Capacity Analysis which have been developed by a number of different NGOs to understand vulnerability to disasters. The V2R approach to analysis shares much in common with these approaches but aims at a fuller, more integrated analysis.

The following sections outline suggested key steps in the process of analysis and offers examples of how V2R analysis can be used in practice. The analysis sections outline suggested checklists of areas to analyse and possible tools to use in your analysis, covering all areas of the framework:

- vulnerability outcome analysis;
- analysis of hazards and stresses;
- livelihoods analysis;
- analysis of future uncertainty;
- governance analysis.

The section on using V2R for action illustrates different ways of using the analysis to achieve different ends, including:

- community planning, a case from Zimbabwe;
- project planning, a case from Nepal;
- reassessing projects, a case from Peru;
- monitoring and evaluation;
- capacity building, cases from Peru and Sri Lanka.

Using the V2R can help to build community capacity to analyse their situation, to actively participate in local development planning and interventions, and to voice their demands or influence wider institutions where appropriate. These sections should serve as a guideline only and can be adapted as appropriate to the context and purpose of each analysis or action.

Participatory processes

V2R analysis and action are intended to be participatory processes which aim to build local capacity and ensure local ownership. Therefore it is important to engage with community members and local leaders to ensure that skills for vulnerability and resilience analysis and action are built for the long term. This might involve developing the capacity of a team of community facilitators to communicate to others the importance of carrying out the analysis and to coordinate activities. After the analysis has been completed, it is essential that the findings are collated and fed back to the whole community, that they have the opportunity to discuss and validate the findings, and that they prioritise areas to take action. It should not be an extractive process to inform decisions which are taken elsewhere, but an informative process to guide local decision making and action.

Whilst encouraging participation, it should be recognized that power relationships exist within communities that can influence the analysis of situations, and decisions on potential solutions. Facilitating discussions with different focus groups or individuals can help ensure that a wide range of perspectives are expressed. Relevant local authorities should also be informed and involved, as they may be able to provide inputs to the analysis as well as support to any resulting plans. It may also encourage them to replicate the planning process in other communities in the future. These might include local government officials responsible for development and for disaster management, government agricultural and livestock staff, and other NGOs or civil society organizations in the area.

Capacities and opportunities

People should not be viewed as helpless in the face of hazards and stresses. Even the poorest have assets and capacity to act. They are also likely to have ideas for opportunities which they would like to pursue to make their lives more resilient. As well as looking at the vulnerable aspects of people's livelihoods and trying to strengthen them, resilience can also be increased by seeking out existing areas of livelihoods capacity or opportunity and building on them. For example, if the community is well organized and some effective and inclusive groups already exist, they may be built on to form disaster preparedness committees, or savings groups. If good and fertile land exists in the community, but groups just lack rights of access to that land or appropriate tools to be able to work that land, then that may present an opportunity for an intervention to improve access. Therefore, in each of the summary tables there is space to include both issues and vulnerabilities, and capacities and opportunities.

Multi-level analysis and action

Even though much of the analysis and action described over the following pages is focused on the community level, this always needs to be complemented with information and inputs from other stakeholders and sources at different levels. During a community analysis, undoubtedly issues will be raised relating to other stakeholders such as government authorities, service providers, and other NGOs. It is important to explore these issues directly with those stakeholders as they may be able to give more information on challenges and opportunities from their perspective and help point towards more appropriate action. For example, community frustration at the lack of extension service provision may be because there are very few local extension staff or they are under resourced. This might point towards the need for collaborative action to demand greater resource provision at a higher level.

3.2 V2R ANALYSIS

The following pages provide questions, tools and processes that can be used in analysing a community's vulnerability and resilience. This analysis does not need to be carried out in a rigid fashion. Flexibility is important and alternative questions and tools can be incorporated at any stage. However, it is recommended that for each stage of the analysis, four main activities are carried out:

- understanding the background and context;
- community level analysis;
- collation and interpretation of the information;
- feedback to the community and other stakeholders.

Understanding the background and context

For each area of analysis it is important to gather background information on the issues and to understand the context. This can either be done before the community analysis or information gathered in the community can be verified or explored through secondary data sources. Local, regional or national information and data sources may complement community level analysis, including government reports and statistics, other NGOs and development agencies, meteorological offices, etc. National and regional hazard and vulnerability monitoring systems include the Famine Early Warning Systems Network (FEWSNET) and Food Insecurity and Vulnerability Information and Mapping (FIVIMS). Difficulties may be faced in collecting secondary data, as information is not always available in suitable or comparable formats, it is not always up to date or consistent in its presentation, and the level of detail or quality may not be adequate. It is therefore important to set aside adequate time for gathering such data and assessing it.

Community level analysis

Each of the following analysis sections outlines some questions to guide community level discussions, and suggests some participatory tools that you can use to explore those questions (described on **Issues Page 5: Participatory tools for analysis**).

Neither the questions or the tools should be treated as a definitive list. Referring back to Part 2 will help to generate more ideas for analysis. It is often useful to explore each issue through a number of different tools with different groups of people (men, women, young, elderly and so on) to ensure that a balanced picture of the whole community is reached. Community level analysis and secondary data collection should complement one another, and differences in what they reveal should be explored not ignored.

Collation and interpretation of the information

Collating and summarising the large amounts of information from secondary sources and from the community analysis can be a challenging and time consuming process. Summary tables have been provided for each stage of the analysis to assist in organizing the information according to the different aspects of the V2R framework. It is important that collation and analysis are done carefully to ensure that the conclusions reached have validity.

Feedback to the community and other stakeholders

It is important that the community is involved in verifying and interpreting the information that they have shared during the process of analysis. The community must understand the overall outcomes of the analysis if they are to develop appropriate plans or take action to address the issues raised (see **Section 3.3**).

Summary sheets of questions, tools and blank tables for each area of analysis can be found in **Section 4.2**.

Issues Page 5. Participatory tools for analysis

There are many participatory tools which can be adapted to suit different contexts and topics for discussion. Their purpose is to engage community members actively in the analysis, rather than it being driven by the facilitator. Large scale visualization methods allow more people to participate and contribute to discussions and using a variety of different tools helps different types of information and experience to be shared. The process of analysis should aim to stimulate reflection and ideas amongst all those involved, rather than simply to extract information. It is often useful to facilitate some discussions with men and women separately to ensure that all voices are heard. The following are brief outlines of participatory tools that could be useful in doing a V2R analysis. For more information on tools for analysis, see Resources.

Mapping

Mapping is a useful tool for identifying geographical areas, buildings, populations or resources that are affected by hazards. Further discussion can reveal the reasons for exposure, and opportunities for reducing exposure. Maps can be used to explore where those with most fragile livelihoods live, physical constraints to their livelihoods, and accessibility of community services. Maps can be drawn on the ground using sticks, stones or leaves, on a blackboard, or on large sheets of paper. Someone should take written notes of the discussion as well as adding relevant information to the map.

Seasonal calendar

Seasonal calendars identify different activities and issues through the year, for example production activities, hazards and stresses, periods of hunger and so on. Use the calendar to stimulate discussion. Who is most affected by the hungry gap? Are seasonal patterns shifting? What are people's coping strategies during stressful times of year?

Source: Practical Action

Discussing local organizations using a venn diagram in North Darfur

Wealth ranking

Wealth ranking helps to identify the characteristics of, or the constraints faced by different wealth groups in a community. Start with three to five categories of well being, for example destitute, very poor, average, doing well and rich and allocate some or all households to the various groups. Discuss the characteristics of people who fall into a particular category, for example land or livestock ownership, income, family size, education, hazard exposure, religion or caste. What are the key constraints faced by the poorest groups and the opportunities to help them to move up?

Drama and story telling

Drama or story telling are useful techniques for getting people to share scenarios of what happens before, during or after a disaster situation. After the drama or story initiate a group discussion about what happened and why. Then discuss how things could be improved if the same situation were to occur again. The drama group could act out another scenario incorporating possible solutions.

Venn diagram

Venn diagrams can identify key service providers within the community and beyond, how important they are, and how accessible they are. Diagrams are made with circles of different sizes and colours placed (as cards) or drawn in relation to one another. The size of circle can represent importance and distance between circles can represent intensity of interaction. Men and women, wealthy and poor, young and old, may well produce different diagrams; the differences are often instructive. Discussions could include challenges in accessing distant but important organizations, which organizations are missing altogether, and changes people would like to see in the future.

Timeline

A timeline generates information about significant events (earthquake, epidemic, landslide, flood, new school building, electricity, new road built, new technology and so on) in the history of the community and their effects or impacts. A timeline is useful to analyse how a conflict situation has evolved. A time trend identifies patterns of change, for example whether flooding is more frequent or severe or whether there are other changing weather patterns. Ensure that older people, both men and women, participate in the discussion. Seeds, stones, sticks or cards can be used to indicate the magnitude of certain events or trends such as floods, crop yields, and so on.

Transect walk / observation

This is a planned walk through the community to observe how people are living and how land is used, asking questions along the way. It can help facilitators to gain a preliminary assessment of local conditions. Direct observation of people, structures, relationships and behaviours, events, and activities also contributes to building up a rich understanding of the community and provides an opening for discussions.

Group discussion

Group discussion is a tool that can be used at any time and in conjunction with most of the participatory methodologies described. The discussion surrounding the use of other tools is often the most enlightening. Sometimes groups can be selected to represent certain sections of the population, for example women, men, youth or elderly, in order to fully explore their perspectives which may otherwise not clearly come out in a mixed group discussion.

Interviews / case studies

Sometimes group based discussion or participatory tools are inappropriate, for example when discussing personal information (for example financial issues, social exclusion or violence), or when one knowledgeable person can provide key information (for example the village chief). In this case individual interviews or case studies are appropriate. Participants should be happy with the degree to which their information will be shared, particularly if it is personal.

Ranking

This tool helps to understand people's priorities or perceptions of importance and it can be done in several ways. Different options (for example hazards or proposed activities) can each be written on a separate card and a group is asked to put them in priority order. Alternatively people can vote by allocating a mark, seed, stone or other small token to their preferred option.

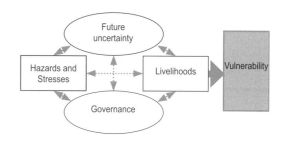

3.2.1 Analysis of vulnerability outcomes

Firstly it is important to build a picture of the key aspects of vulnerability experienced in the community or by particularly vulnerable groups or households. As described in **Section 2.1**, vulnerable households and communities tend to experience disasters, they are less able to adapt to change, they often experience uncomfortable periods of food insecurity, and as a result they struggle to move out of poverty. At the outset of the analysis it is useful to identify which of these key aspects of vulnerability is relevant, how prevalent they are in the community and which groups are most at risk. These will then be explored in more detail in the subsequent aspects of the analysis, keeping a strong focus on those groups identified as vulnerable in different ways.

What to ask about vulnerability outcomes?

- What is the history of disasters in the community?
- Are there other events, circumstances or trends that they feel unable to cope with or adapt to?
- Are there households or social / livelihood groups which suffer periods of food insecurity?
- How do members of the community assess wealth (assets, education, inclusion, etc) and which social or livelihood groups are identified as poorest or unable to move out of poverty?

Suggested tools to use

- Secondary data: gather external data on disasters, livelihoods, food security and so on, in the area.

- Transect walk: make observations about the community, its resources and infrastructure, and general wellbeing of people.

- Timeline: understand broad history of disasters in the community or changes that they have had to adapt to.

- Key informant interviews: find out from community leaders about the different social and livelihood groups in the community, and their perceptions of their relative vulnerability.

- Wealth ranking: understand local indicators of poverty. Identify poorest and food insecure groups.

Table 7. Collating the information on vulnerability outcomes

History of disasters	• ongoing conflict throughout living memory • bad droughts and famine 1983-85, 1987-88, 1990-91, 2000-01, 2004-05
Other events or trends	• increasing availability of arms leading to more violence • more frequent drought (1 in 5 years) • more men migrating
Groups suffering food insecurity	• most suffer from food insecurity during drought • in other years households with fewer livestock suffered seasonal hunger • food and livestock stolen during raids further contributing to seasonal hunger
Groups living in poverty	• households with fewer livestock considered poorest • women-headed households (many husbands killed in conflict) • households with many young / children

Source: Katherine Pasteur, Practical Action

Creating a timeline of vulnerabiltiy outcomes, Bangladesh

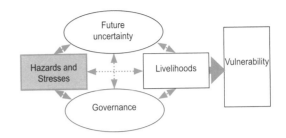

3.2.2 Analysis of hazards and stresses

Ideally we want to gather as much information as possible about the different types of hazards and stresses that impact on different groups within the community as well as the community as a whole. We also want to know about the extent of their exposure, or any measures they are already taking to improve their disaster preparedness.

What to ask about hazards and stresses?

Building on the information about disasters and other causes of vulnerability mentioned in the outcome analysis, identify the different hazards and stresses that have affected the community or particular groups in living memory, both regular occurrences and one-offs. Think beyond typical natural hazards, to include biological, economic, socio-political and other hazards and stresses. Then explore the nature of the hazards and stresses themselves, as well as the links to livelihoods, future uncertainty, and governance factors, using the following questions and tools. Be aware that people tend to identify more recent events as the most significant and to overestimate their impact as compared to earlier ones. For a reminder of some of these issues, see **Section 2.3**.

- What is the typical frequency and duration of occurrence of this hazard or stress? Is it seasonal? Has it changed over time, for example due to climate change or other trends?
- What is the speed of onset of the hazard or stress? Are there any warning signs? Are there established early warning systems?
- Are there any underlying causes of the hazard or stress? Does the community understand them, or know how to address them?
- Which groups within the community (livelihood groups, social groups, geographical groups, people with disability, etc) are most affected and how?
- Which community or individual assets, property, or services are affected (for example infrastructure, services, markets, crops, savings, land) and how?
- How do different groups typically respond immediately after the hazard occurs (are there contingency plans, safe areas, emergency resources, response organizations, etc)?
- Based on the issues raised, what opportunities and capacities are available, or could be strengthened to improve peoples' disaster preparedness?

Suggested tools

- Secondary data: gather external data on hazards and vulnerable groups from relevant sources.
- Hazard map: identify geographical areas that are physically vulnerable for example to flood, landslide, etc.
- Hazard trend analysis: a development of the time line to better understand changes in hazard frequency, severity, or predictability over time. May be linked to climate change.
- Story telling: find out how people typically behave or respond after a hazard.
- Group discussion: discuss capacities and opportunities for improved disaster preparedness. Separate groups discussions with men and women may reveal differences in interests and capacities.

Table 8. Collating the information on hazards and stresses

Hazard priority 1: drought	Issues and vulnerabilities	Capacities and opportunities for resilience
Frequency, duration, seasonality, trends	Every 3 to 5 years. Used to be less frequent in the past. Increasingly severe, maybe due to climate change.	
Warning signs, early warning	No formal early warning systems; some are aware of biophysical signs such as migration of birds.	Early warning from metrological organizations would help.
Underlying causes	• Misuse of land, deforestation and climate change • Some tree planting has taken place but not significant • Don't know what causes climate change or how to address it	• Reforestation could be more widespread • Need more information about climate change and its impacts
Groups affected	• All households dependent on farming affected by loss of crops and income. • Smallholder farmers without water sources most affected. • Households with no family to assist them • Female headed households badly affected due to lack of husband support	Soil and water conservation could be improved.
Assets and services affected	• Water resources dry up; some conflict • Crops die, especially vegetables. • Animals die • Food aid enters market and undermines prices for remaining producers. • Schools close as teachers return to town	• Need to better manage scarce water resources • Community leaders try to organize support to the most affected
Immediate response	• No response strategy • In severe droughts food aid is available to the most vulnerable	Planning and preparedness for drought could help

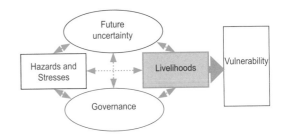

3.2.3 Livelihood analysis

A livelihoods analysis should explore in detail the characteristics of the groups that are least able to cope and recover when hazards and stresses occur (see **Section 2.4**). Although the whole community may be affected, it is particularly important to identify those whose livelihoods are least able to support them and help them get back on track. Try to identify specific groups of people rather than very broad groups (for example 'small scale farmers with less than two hectares of land, dependent on rain-fed agriculture', rather than just 'farmers').

What to ask about livelihoods?

What are the principal livelihood groups within the community, and which of these groups are identified as socio-economically vulnerable or unable to cope and recover when a particular hazard or stress occurs?

- What kinds of coping strategies (erosive or non-erosive) do different people currently use when they are affected by hazards or stresses (particularly vulnerable livelihood groups).
- What are the key constraints and opportunities faced by each vulnerable livelihood group (for example organizational capacity, access to productive resources, access to skills and technologies, access to markets, secure living conditions)?
- Are their livelihoods affected by particular hazards, by climate change, or by other long term trends which should be explored further?
- What are the gaps and opportunities in relation to external institutions which affect their livelihoods (services, financial, safety nets?)

Suggested tools

- Secondary data: gather external data on principal livelihoods, resource constraints, markets, employment opportunities, service providers etc. in the area.
- Seasonal calendar: use to identify the livelihood activities throughout the year, and the different stresses or hazards that affect the resilience of those livelihoods.
- Ranking: focus group discussion with community leaders can identify principal livelihood groups in the community and which are identified as poor or vulnerable.
- Key informant or group interviews representing different livelihood groups identified as vulnerable.

Table 9. Collating the information on livelihoods (based on Case Study 2)

	Livelihood vulnerabilities and erosive coping strategies *(governance aspects in italic)*	Coping capacities and opportunities for resilience *(governance aspects in italic)*
Community organization	• Many people have left the community, for example so their children can attend school or to find more work. • Community and institutions have become weakened as the population declines. • *External links to possible support organizations are very weak, and skills to apply for funds are poor.*	• Good mayor who is keen to act for the community. • *Some government safety net pro-grammes such as Glass of Milk.* • *Need to strengthen skills and external networks of community organizations.*
Access to productive resources	• Land holdings small (2 ha per family). Limits the quantity and variety of crops produced. • The growing season is short. Rain-fed agriculture is limited to one harvest per year. • Poor animal health and low productivity. • Farmers unable to protect crops from frosts which are more unseasonal due to climate change. • *No agricultural or animal health support services (government, private or NGO).* • *No awareness raising about climate change or how to cope.*	• Need more agricultural skills development. • Crop diversification. • Animal health and breed improvement. • Improved water management • *Extension or training providers needed.*
Skills and Technologies	• Education levels are low as only basic primary is available in the community • *Little investment in education* • Lack of knowledge about technologies or methods to protect crops from unseasonal frost. • *No information or advisory services to the community.* • Limited access to larger scale irrigation which could extend the growing season. • *Unable to access funds for projects such as improved irrigation.*	• School buses. • Agricultural skills development. • Access to irrigation skills and technologies. • *Extension or training providers needed.* • *External funding needed.*
Access to markets and employment	• The market is some distance from parts of the community. • Cost of transporting low value crops to market is high. • Few local livelihood options beyond basic agriculture. • Casual labour is not considered desirable as it takes men from the community. • *Participatory budget resources exist in the municipality but not available to fund production related projects.*	• Eco-tourism could provide non-farm employment. • Better market understanding to select good cash crops. • *Training in non-farm livelihoods needed.* • *Training needed in accessing markets.* • *Access to participatory budget process.*
Safe living conditions	Some vulnerability of houses and animals from landslides.	Tree planting to reduce run-off.

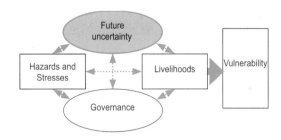

3.2.4 Analysing future uncertainty

The analysis of long-term trends is important to help in understanding significant changes over time that are contributing to people's vulnerability, and how those trends might continue or change in the future. Some past trends may already have been raised in the hazard analysis or livelihood analysis. It is important to consider the possible impact of these trends into the future, and how people will adapt to those anticipated changes, whether they are certain or not. See **Section 2.5** for a reminder of different long term trends that might be relevant, including climate change, and the relevance of adaptive capacity. They can be explored further in this aspect of the analysis.

What to ask about long term trends including climate change?

- What significant trends or changes have people observed in recent decades, and how do they expect them to evolve in the future? What secondary data exists on past and future trends?
- What are the impacts and implications of these trends on people's livelihoods and the incidence of hazards?
- How do people understand the causes of these trends or changes?
- Do people have access to relevant and timely information to help them adapt to those changes (for example future predictions, short term forecasting and adaptation strategies)?
- How are people adapting to change now? Do they have the necessary resources to be able to adapt (for example organizational capacity, access to productive resources, access to skills and technologies, access to markets, secure living conditions)?
- Do they feel confident about their ability to adapt to future changes?
- What institutional response has there been to the trends identified (awareness-raising, mitigation, support, information and funding for adaptation)?
- What opportunities are there for influencing these trends, improving understanding, ensuring access to information and resources, and building confidence to adapt?

Suggested tools

- Secondary data: collect external data on climate, economic and other trends and impacts.
- Long term trend analysis: explore the historical patterns of issues that affect development, including social, economic, institutional and environmental issues over periods of between 10 and 40 years.
- Knowledge network mapping: explore different sources of information relating to climate change or other trends (for example medium term climate predictions, expected trends in crop or energy prices, technologies for climate adaptation, etc) using a venn diagram.
- Story telling and discussion: allow people to share experiences of how their livelihoods have been impacted by trends (such as climate change) and how they have attempted to cope or adapt. Discuss ways in which they could be better supported to adapt in the future.

Table 10. Collating the information on future uncertainty (based on Case Study 3)

Trend: climate change	Issues and vulnerabilities *(governance aspects in italic)*	Capacities and opportunities for resilience *(governance aspects in italic)*
Observed changes	• Increasing drought. • Unusual rainfall patterns. • Rainstorms decreasing in number but increasing in intensity. • Overall increase in precipitation and average temperature. • Expectation extremes will continue to increase.	
Impacts	• Increase in hazards such as landslides, flash floods, wind storms and hail. • Erosion leading to decreased soil fertility and lower productivity. • Scarcity of water for irrigation during dry season leading to lower productivity. • Inability to follow traditional cropping and harvesting patterns.	
Understanding	• Some recognition of climate change, but little understanding of how to address it and how it will change over time. • Feeling that they have no control over the future climate.	• Awareness-raising about climate change in schools. • Forest conservation to reduce landslides and erosion as climate change brings more intense rainfall.
Access to information	• No new information available about how to adapt to changes. • Little access to weather forecasts. • Little access to support institutions for any kind of training.	• *Better early warning or forecasting from government institutions.* • *Training on agricultural diversification – vegetables, fruit, goat production.* • *One district based NGO exists with agricultural training capacity.*
Existing adaptation strategies	None mentioned	Those with more diversified farms (crops and animals) were coping better.

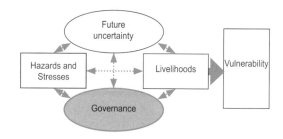

3.2.5 Governance analysis

It is important to understand the roles played by different organizations both within and outside the community, how accessible they are, and how they are contributing to improvements in the community (see **Section 2.6**). We also need to identify organizations and other stakeholders that are not currently available to the community but who could be helping. It is also necessary to identify groups or individuals and government policies that are creating constraints on the community and limiting their opportunities for improvement. The aim of the governance analysis is to identify some of the factors that are underlying the livelihood analysis and hazard analysis, so it is important to refer back to issues that were raised and explore them in more detail during this analysis. Not only local, but also national or even international level policies and institutions may be playing a role. It will be necessary to complement the community analysis with discussions and interviews with stakeholders outside the community such as district, regional and even national level government and NGO staff.

What to ask about governance?

Look back at the key issues raised in previous steps in the analysis. Have vulnerabilities relating to governance environments already been raised?

- Which organizations, policies, processes or underlying systemic issues are contributing to the occurrence of hazards, exposure to hazards, livelihood vulnerability, or future uncertainty? How or why are those organizations or policies contributing to vulnerability?
- Which organizations, policies or processes could help enable disaster preparedness, strengthen, livelihood security and diversification, or adaptive capacity?
- What opportunities exist for improving the governance environment: ensuring decentralized and participatory decision making, strengthening local to national links, promoting integrated approaches or addressing systemic issues?

Suggested tools

- Secondary data: collect external data on locally relevant organizations, policies, processes etc.
- Venn diagrams: use to map different livelihood and disaster preparedness service providers and their accessibility by the community as a starting point for discussion on institutional gaps and opportunities. Venn diagrams can also be used to map other types of actors within the community and the strength of relationships can be assessed by different thickness of lines drawn between them.
- Interviews: with key informants such as local government, NGO and private sector service providers to provide further insight into institutional limitations
- Market mapping: identify the different market chain actors and business environment factors and the various linkages between primary producers and final consumers to help identify bottlenecks and opportunities (see **Issues Page 2**).

Table 11. Collating the information on governance

	Issues and vulnerabilities	Capacities and opportunities for resilience
Hazards and disaster preparedness	Zimbabwe National Water Authority should manage flood and drought forecasting but skills, technologies and funds are lacking.	People have become aware of the need for proper forecasting.
	District Drought Management Committee exists and is considered important, but lacking in clear roles and capacity.	Opportunity to build DDMC capacity for integrated disaster risk reduction.
	Locally operating NGOs respond to disasters with targeted humanitarian relief / food aid / food for work.	Targeting approach of NGOs (for example based on livestock ownership) is not favoured by households who prefer block targeting.
		Department of Social Welfare responds in severe droughts with grain loan and assistance with school fees.
Livelihoods	Department of Vet Services and AGRITEX lack resources for training. DVS distributes drugs late during disease outbreaks.	There are some examples of good partnership working with NGOs who have more resources.
	District Development Fund lacks resources to maintain road network, with implications for transportation of food to and from markets.	
	Farmers are unclear about title deeds for land acquired under land reforms so they are hesitant to invest in developing their farms.	Ministry of Lands could be lobbied to speed up provision of title deeds.
Future uncertainty	Climate change is resulting in declining crop yields but there is no institutional or policy focus on this.	More climate awareness is needed amongst all institutional stakeholders and policy responses developed, for example more training on water harvesting.
	Grain marketing policies favour maize production which does poorly in semi arid areas, and will do worse in the future under climate change	More focus is needed on drought tolerant crops. Awareness-raising is needed at policy level.

Sources: Bongo, P. (2006) *Disaster Management in Zimbabwe and Institutional Analysis;*
Ndlovu, S. (2009) *An Institutional Analysis of Drought, Reducing Drought Risks in Bulilima and Mangwe*

3.3 FROM ANALYSIS TO ACTION

The V2R framework and analysis can be applied in a range of different situations. Once secondary data collection and field based analysis is complete, the full findings should be consolidated, and where necessary, verified by the community. The consolidation of results will involve bringing together the five tables that were produced to collate the different areas of analysis (Tables 7 to 11 in Section 3.2). These should be looked at collectively to identify the linkages and relationships between the different areas of analysis, and the key issues emerging. Based on these key issues from the analyses, and with reference back to the detailed Resilience Framework (Figure 7), priority areas of vulnerability and opportunities resilience should be identified. From the basis of those priority issues an appropriate action plan can begin to be developed.

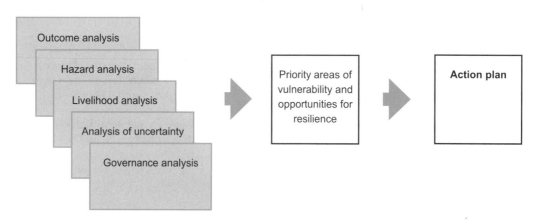

Figure 6. Moving from analysis to action planning

The following sections detail case studies illustrating how the V2R can be used in practice, drawing on Practical Action's country programme experience. Three examples are based on using V2R analysis to contribute to planning or adapting projects in different contexts. Two further case studies illustrate other ways in which the V2R framework can be used: for monitoring and evaluation, and for capacity building.

The different examples are as follows:

- V2R for community planning, a case from Zimbabwe;
- V2R for NGO project planning, a case from Nepal;
- V2R for incorporating climate change, a case from Peru;
- V2R for monitoring and evaluation, a case from Bangladesh;
- V2R for capacity building, cases from Peru and Sri Lanka.

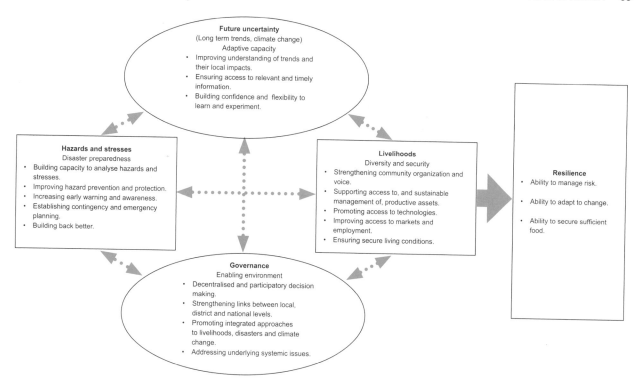

Figure 7. The detailed resilience framework

3.3.1 V2R for community planning – a case from Zimbabwe

Drawing on a participatory V2R analysis, communities can be facilitated in the process of turning the identified priorities into local action plans, which may be implemented with their own resources or with support from external organizations. Community plans should be realistic and attention should be paid to where resources will come from for implementation, the time frame for achieving objectives, and ensuring that the most vulnerable will benefit most.

From analysis to community action

It is important to carry out action planning soon after the V2R analysis took place so that people are still engaged and interested in addressing the concerns they raised. For practical reasons, it may be unrealistic to include all members in the planning process, in which case representatives of different community groups should be present and plans should be fed back to all members for approval. Ideally the process should be led by a VDC, or other inclusive local institution. Local government officials who were involved in the V2R analysis should also be included at the planning stage, or plans should be discussed with them later, as they may be able to provide support in terms of staff and resources.

The community should be encouraged to think of some priority strategies and projects for addressing the areas of vulnerability identified in the V2R analysis. These should include immediate actions, short term strategies and some longer term actions. It is also useful to ensure that there is a mix of actions which can be achieved with internal resources and those which require external support or influencing. Responsibilities and time frames should be allocated to each activity or project, and some form of monitoring decided upon (see **Section 3.3.4**). The Community Based Planning (CBP) methodology, developed by Practical Action and other partners in Southern Africa, can be referred to for more ideas for this stage (Gumbo, 2009).

An integrated community development plan from Buvuma Ward 18

In Buvuma Ward 18, Gwanda District, Zimbabwe the key hazards and stresses that were identified in the V2R analysis were drought, HIV and Aids and livestock diseases. Principal livelihood challenges were in part related to these hazards - drought and livestock disease were affecting yields in part due to a lack of skills for improving and commercializing food and livestock production for better nutrition and for increasing incomes. Long term trends include the growing prevalence of HIV and Aids, the increasing frequency of drought (linked to climate change), loss of seed diversity, and an increasingly tough economic environment. Governance issues identified include the lack of capacity and resources of AGRITEX (agricultural extension services) to support communities, the poor management capacity of many self help groups, but the opportunity provided by several NGOs working in the area.

After considering the results of the V2R analysis, the community identified a number of priority areas for activity which are summarised in Box 1 below. These were then turned into action plans, assigning responsibilities, identifying specific beneficiaries, identifying inputs required from other stakeholders and setting a time frame.

Box 1. Selected activities from Buvuma Ward 18 community development and disaster management plan

The following activities were identified through the V2R process to address problems associated with drought, livestock disease and HIV and Aids in Buvuma Ward 18.

- Grow more drought tolerant varieties to ensure harvest even when rains are poor.
- Improve crop storage to ensure food supply between harvests.
- Develop in-field rainwater harvesting including dead level contours, infiltration pits and improved rainwater storage facilities to reduce impacts of drought.
- Reduce livestock disease through use of vaccinations and herbal treatments supported by training local paravets.
- Encourage behaviour change to reduce HIV and Aids and promote herbal gardening and use of other traditional immunity boosters.
- Develop community based goat breeding scheme and produce more home grown feeds from crop residues to improve income from small livestock.
- Pilot a small livestock pass on scheme for vulnerable households for example HIV and AIDS-affected households.
- Establish nutritional gardens for growing, processing and marketing vegetables to improve household nutrition and incomes.
- Establish links with meteorological service for drought early warning.
- Select and train disaster management committee to oversee all activities.
- Share plans with relevant sections of local government, for example veterinary extension department to request training to paravets and support access to improved goat breeds.
- Strengthen links and share plans with local disaster response agencies, both government and NGO.

3.3.2 V2R for NGO project planning – a case from Nepal

The V2R framework and analysis can be used for appraisal to guide larger scale NGO project planning. Again, a process is needed to bring together the analysis, prioritise areas for action, and to design an appropriate set of activities to build resilience. This does not necessarily mean including activities which address *all* aspects of the framework – proposed actions should respond to prioritised areas of the framework to achieve balanced progress towards strengthening resilience. Clearly, an NGO facilitated project will have more resources available and greater opportunity to influence the governance environment at various levels.

From analysis to project planning

Priority areas for action will tend to be developed into a Logical Framework (log frame), or other planning framework, to help describe the contribution of proposed activities to achieving the desired outcomes and impacts. Table 12 illustrates a generic log frame, which can be built upon with the contextual detail of a local analysis. It is important to design indicators to monitor the achievement of impacts and outcomes, and these will be looked at in the upcoming **Section 3.3.4**.

Throughout **Section 2** many examples of activities have been cited which would contribute to the different resilience outcomes. The proposed actions should not be short term solutions but should aim to tackle underlying causes of vulnerability. This will mean ensuring action to address future uncertainty (see **Section 2.5**) and the various elements of the governance environment (see **Section 2.6**). Activities should be realistic and attainable with the resources and time frame of any project or programme.

Table 12. Generic logical framework for a project to strengthen resilience	
Goal	Poor people in fragile, rural areas enabled to build resilient livelihoods as a result of better access to skills and technologies to manage agriculture and natural resources, increased capacity to manage hazards and increased ability to adapt to climatic and economic changes.
Impacts	*Food secure:* able to obtain sufficient, nutritious, appropriate food throughout the year. *Able to manage risk:* disaster preparedness strategies in place and losses from hazards reduced. *Able to adapt to future changes:* able to draw on resources and information to make changes in response to impacts of climatic and economic trends. *Able to move out of poverty:* greater security, assets, income or livelihood options.
Outcomes	*Increased security and diversity of livelihoods:* improved access resources, skills, technologies, markets, organizational capacity and secure living conditions. *Capacity for and implementation of disaster preparedness:* analysis, prevention, protection, early warning and planning carried out. *Adaptive capacity strengthened:* understanding of trends, access to information, and confidence to adapt improved. *More enabling governance environment:* greater access to local services, supported by relevant, integrated policies.
Activities	The outcomes are achieved through project activities such as training courses, demonstrations, building dams, facilitation, influencing, and so on. This is the detailed level of each project and will vary from project to project.

Activities for resilience outcomes in Chitwan, Nepal

Communities in the Chitwan District of Nepal are feeling the effects of climate change in terms of increased weather-related hazards such as flood, wind storms, hail, and so on. As **Case Study 3** illustrates, this trend of worsening hazards is leading to significant new impacts on lives and livelihoods, including human deaths, loss of livestock and crops, damage to homes and infrastructure, reduced food availability, and temporary disruption in access to services such as markets, health centres and schools.

Through a process of community led analysis and prioritisation, a number of key areas for action were identified to address these vulnerabilities and to strengthen community resilience, not only to climate change, but to more regular hazards and other trends. These activities focussed on strengthening natural resource based livelihoods, assessing climate related hazards and improving preparedness, raising awareness amongst a range of stakeholders around climate impacts on livelihoods, and influencing at various levels to increase support to community based adaptation. The specific activities are outlined in the log frame below (Table 13).

Table 13. Log frame summary: increasing the resilience of poor communities to cope with the impact of climate change, Nepal (2004–2007)

Outcomes	Activities
Capacity for and implementation of disaster preparedness	• Strengthen the capacity of local communities to build physical protection structures to cope with climate hazards. • Strengthen early warning systems by enabling the provision of relevant climate information for local people. • Establish participatory planning processes with community groups to identify and prioritise disaster preparedness plans. • Establish a task force of community, local government, NGOs and private sector to link local preparedness into wider development plans.

Increased security and diversity of livelihoods	• Community-led identification and prioritisation of natural resource management options and technologies.
	• Based on community priorities, facilitate training in sustainable natural resource-based technologies and techniques such as:
	  o conservation farming methods
	  o watershed management and hillside reforestation
	  o water harvesting and rehabilitation of local irrigation
	  o identification and promotion of income generating activities – e.g. processing medicinal herbs and vegetable solar drying.

Adaptive capacity strengthened	• Community assessment of local knowledge and perceptions of climatic conditions, interactions with farming systems, biodiversity and water resources and capacity to adapt. • Develop awareness raising of climate change and its impacts on livelihoods amongst communities, NGOs and officials. • Capacity building of local CBOs, NGOs and local authorities to analyse and monitor risks to livelihoods from climate change and to incorporate actions into long-term development plans.
More enabling governance environment	• Bring together policymakers, influencers and donors with local communities to allow them to see concrete evidence of community-led adaptation measures. • Disseminate best practices and policy messages to local, regional, national and international stakeholders. • Develop innovative proposals for engaging the international community in support of community-based adaptation.

3.3.3 V2R for incorporating climate change – a case from Peru

The V2R framework and analysis can be used to look at either existing or new areas of work to understand the possible impacts of climate change, and potential for building adaptive capacity (see **Section 2.5**). This is important as climate change may not have been considered relevant or given priority when existing projects were designed, but impacts may be becoming significant as the project develops. Furthermore, increasingly funding is becoming available for projects and programmes which specifically aim to address the impacts of climate change and build adaptive capacity. Such projects should take a holistic approach, as the V2R encourages.

Climate vulnerability and resilience analysis

Carrying out analysis of climate vulnerability does not mean looking only at future uncertainty and ignoring other elements of the framework. It means exploring all aspects of the framework but with a stronger focus on climate change as the most significant long term trend contributing to vulnerability. If climate trends are leading to greater incidence of hazards, then those should be explored under hazard analysis, including warning signs, groups and assets affected, and response strategies. It is important, too, to understand which livelihood groups are most affected by climate change, or may be most affected if this trend continues. What are the constraints faced by these livelihood groups, how are they being affected, and what opportunities exist to strengthen their resilience through improved organizational capacity, management of natural resources, access to skills and technologies, access to markets, and secure living conditions.

Using V2R for climate adaptation actions in Peru

Climate vulnerability and resilience analysis can feed into planning action to strengthen adaptive capacity. In the Ancash region of Peru, the results of a climate vulnerability and resilience analysis were incorporated into an existing disaster risk reduction project which had not previously focused on climate change impacts (refer back to **Case Study 2** and **Section 3.2.2**). The following paragraphs describe activities added to the project to ensure resilience in the face of climate change was enhanced.

Disaster preparedness. The project initially had a strong focus on disaster preparedness, building capacity for hazard analysis, supporting activities to reduce hazards such as landslides resulting from heavy rainfall by reforesting slopes, developing emergency plans and evacuation routes in case of earthquakes, and managing the stress of seasonal water shortages. The weather related hazards and stresses are likely to become more extreme under climate change and therefore these preparedness activities would continue to be pertinent. Early warning systems are now being established for unseasonal frosts.

Livelihoods diversity and security. Existing project activities had aimed to improve the diversity and security of livelihoods, through activities such as improved irrigation systems, strengthening small livestock production and increased production of vegetables for consumption and sale. Climate vulnerability analysis revealed that many farmers were still unable to adapt to more frequent and unseasonal frosts which were affecting crops. A response to this was the reintroduction of lost potato diversity. Farmers are now growing a range of different potato varieties in one field, and observing which are more resistant to frost, to drought or to heavy rains, in order to maintain a mix that ensures a harvest whatever adverse weather they experience.

Adaptive capacity. In order to build capacity of households and the community as a whole to make appropriate changes to their livelihoods in response to changing conditions, it was necessary to strengthen their understanding of climate change, improve their access to information that would help them to adapt, and build their confidence and flexibility to learn and change. An important activity was building the capacity of resilient farmer leaders. Their training covered issues relating to the causes and effects of climate change, as well as different strategies for strengthening and adapting livelihoods, specifically to cope with climate impacts. By developing the capacity of farmer leaders in the target communities, the people would be able to draw on their skills and support over time to help them to experiment and implement the different adaptation options that they knew about. These leaders would also serve as a link to other institutions that could update them with further ideas and information over time.

An enabling governance environment. Analysis revealed that institutional support to communities around climate change was lacking or inappropriate. Practical Action is now working more closely with local authorities to raise their awareness of the key issues relating to climate change, how communities will be affected, and how they can be supported to adapt. They are participating in the development of a Regional Climate Change Strategy with other stakeholders, which will include greater focus on supporting community based adaptation.

Source: Practical Action Latin America

Graduates from the School of Resilient Farmer Leaders, Ancash Peru

3.3.4 V2R for monitoring and evaluation – a case from Bangladesh

Monitoring and evaluation (M&E) is an essential element of the project or programme cycle in order to assess the effectiveness of the actions taken. The V2R framework and analysis can be used to guide M&E to ensure that progress towards resilience is being achieved. Indicators can be based around the different elements highlighted within the framework (**Section 2**), and they can be monitored using questions and methods suggested in the analysis section (**Section 3**).

Key elements of monitoring and evaluation

Depending on the size or scope of an activity, project, or programme to be monitored and evaluated, the details of the system that is developed will differ. However, the following are some basic elements of any M&E system:

- Indicators of success based on the different activities to be undertaken, the outcomes to be achieved and the impacts in terms of achieving resilience.
- Tools or methods for monitoring and evaluation, ensuring that they are suitable in terms of complexity and time required for information collection.
- Appropriate baseline data, based on the indicators, so that changes over time can be compared to the initial situation.
- Allocation of responsibilities and time frames so that reflection and learning occurs on a regular basis, not only at the end of the project.

It is advisable to keep M&E systems as simple as possible. There is a tendency to become over-ambitious and to collect large amounts of baseline and monitoring data, without thinking through how the data will be used later to monitor outcomes and impact. An approach based on simple tools clearly linked to a limited number of useful indicators is likely to be more achievable and therefore more successful in the long run. Participatory tools, including those outlined in on **Issues Page 5: Participatory Tools for Analysis**, are recommended as a means of directly involving community members in M&E, drawing on their local knowledge and perceptions. What is most important in any M&E system is to ensure a process of critical reflection around which actions are successful in reducing vulnerability in order to continually improve practice, rather than simply collect data and tick boxes.

Indicators for resilience

The V2R framework can be used to help identify a range of indicators against which to measure progress towards resilience. There are at least three levels of indicators that can be measured: activities, outcomes and impacts. The following two tables (14 and 15) contain suggested indicators at outcome and impact levels, which draw on the different elements of the V2R framework. The first table is based on an example from Bangladesh which did not have a strong focus on adaptive capacity at the time of design, though some elements have been added. Further indicators relating to disaster resilience (though with less focus on climate change) can be derived from John Twigg's useful publication: *Characteristics of a Disaster Resilient Community: A Guidance note'* (Twigg, 2007).

Table 14. Examples of outcome indicators based on the project Mainstreaming Livelihood-Centred Approaches to Disaster Management 2006–2010 in Gaibanda, Bangladesh

Outcomes	Example indicators
Disaster preparedness	• Three project locations have analysed their community vulnerability and resilience. • Five communities have disaster management plans. • Five CBOs are functioning and active in disaster preparedness. • Five communities have functioning early warning committees to alert them of flood. • Three rescue boats are available for rescue and evaluation during an emergency.
Diverse and secure livelihoods	• 37 mutual assistance groups are supporting community livelihood activities. • Ten per cent of beneficiaries practice hazard resistant agricultural technologies (floating garden, zero tillage cultivation, early planting). • Ten per cent of beneficiaries have non-farm livelihood skills. • 135 homeless families have hazard resilient houses. • 15 per cent of beneficiaries can access raised tube wells during flood.
Adaptive capacity	• 20 per cent of beneficiaries are aware of climate change and its impacts . • 20 per cent of beneficiaries can access information about at least 10 types of on farm and off farm activities. • 15 per cent of beneficiaries have established new networks with service providers.
Enabling environment	• Government service providers have stronger linkages with communities as a result of providing 150 orientation sessions. • Union, Upazilla and District government staff are aware of project approach and lessons. • Humanitarian organizations working in the district are more aware of livelihood centred risk reduction approaches. • National and international stakeholders have accessed case studies from Bangladesh illustrating best practice in integrated approaches to achieving resilience.

Table 15. Generic impact indicators of resilience

Impacts	Example indicators
Ability to manage hazards	• Increase in protection of assets. • Reduced loss of life and productive assets for example reduction in livestock lost due to drought/flood.
Ability to adapt to change	New initiatives taken by people in response to change, for example using weather forecasts or changing crops/animals/water use.
Food security	• Decrease in length of hunger gap for people. • Increase to three adequate meals all year round. • Decrease in malnutrition measurements.

3.3.5 V2R for capacity building – cases from Peru and Sri Lanka

The previous sections have illustrated that the V2R approach has relevance in several different contexts, and can be used by different stakeholders, from communities, to NGOs and government decision makers at all levels. Some degree of capacity building is likely to be necessary in order to familiarise these users with the reasoning behind taking an integrated approach, the details of the different elements to be integrated (i.e. hazards and stresses, livelihoods, future uncertainty, and governance), and the practicalities of analysing and addressing the various elements.

Using the V2R for capacity building

This document can be used as a guide for training on the V2R approach and carrying out a V2R analysis. **Part 2** provides content and case studies for training, and exercises for field practice can also be incorporated, based on **Part 3**. The actual delivery of capacity building or training will differ a lot according to the audience so a generalized approach cannot be described. It is important to understand clearly the needs and interests of the audience and tailor the detail of the messages, the length of training and the style of delivery to suit.

The selection of content for any training will also depend on the background, or 'starting point' of the audience. Training for disaster or climate specialists may require more time to be spent on livelihood and governance aspects, and vice versa. Time should be taken to assess the needs of potential participants, the gaps in their knowledge, and how they are likely to use the knowledge in practice, before designing a training.

The training does not necessarily need to follow the same order as the elements set out in this document – any part can be used as an entry point. Similarly, capacity building to community or CBO members will be very different in style and content to working with national level policy makers. For the former, thinking about the different elements of the V2R in an integrated way is likely to be second nature, but seeing these in the form of a diagrammatic representation may be unfamiliar. Learning practical skills for analysis and planning are also likely to be more relevant to their needs. Policymakers with a university education may find an integrated framework easy to grasp in theory, but may not have thought through the implications for organizational practices at different levels.

Table 16. Tailoring training to different audiences

Who	What	How
Community leaders or community as a whole	• Basic concepts of integrated approach. • How to carry out integrated analysis and planning.	• Give practical explanations and illustrations. • Facilitated process of carrying out analysis and planning.
Project staff, local CBOs, local NGOs, local government	• Concepts of integrated approach in detail. • Relevance of integrated approach to projects / local development. • Skills for facilitating analysis. • Implications for organizational practice.	• Presentations, group discussion of case studies, reflection on personal experience and so on. • Field visit to carry out analysis and learn facilitation skills.
Decision makers, policymakers at regional and national levels	• Concepts of integrated approach in detail. • Relevance of integrated approach to policy. • Implications of integrated approach for policy and practice.	• Presentations, group discussions of case studies, reflections on personal experience of integrated policy and so on. • Field visits to see local level realities.

The length of training will depend again on the audience and how much time they need to understand the topics in theory, and whether practical analysis or field visits will be incorporated. Spending some time in the field – whether carrying out a full V2R analysis, or merely talking informally with households and community leaders – can be an extremely valuable learning experience for most types of audience.

Examples of training on V2R

Practical Action has developed some country specific training resources and carried out capacity building around taking a livelihoods centred approach to disaster risk reduction, combining different elements of the V2R framework according to the focus of different projects or audience needs (see **Resources**). Some examples and lessons are outlined here.

A five-day training was carried out with Practical Action country office staff in 2008 in order to strengthen understanding of sustainable livelihoods and supporting access to markets amongst staff typically working on disaster risk reduction, and raise awareness of disaster risk issues amongst staff working on market strengthening for livelihoods. The training aimed to achieve a balance between theory and practice as illustrated in Box 2.

Box 2. Training schedule used in a staff training in Peru in 2008

Days 1–2: classroom based
- Presentation of the different elements that make up the V2R framework,
- Group discussion by participants to draw on their own experiences to explore and challenge the issues.
- Discussion of relevance of V2R to different areas of work across programmes

Days 3–5: mixture of classroom and field based
- Discussion use of V2R for field analysis, including the practicalities of using PRA tools
- Field visits to carry out household based analysis in a community and market analysis in a market place.
- Reflection on field experiences.
- Discussion of use of V2R for monitoring and evaluation including design of monitoring indicators for a local project.

In Sri Lanka the concept of Decentralized Disaster Risk Management (DDRM) has been promoted by Practical Action since early 2000. The importance of local governments in disaster risk reduction is increasingly recognized. In this context, Practical Action has developed a substantial training manual on DDRM for local government representatives, which can be drawn on to develop courses or workshops for different audiences (Practical Action South Asia, 2010). It has often been challenging to bring participants together to a central location for trainings that last several days. Courses have therefore been decentralized and are targeted to particular stakeholders groups (elected members, planners and communities) to ensure a high degree of relevance.

PART 4
ANNEXES

4.1 FRAMEWORKS AND MODELS

4.1.1 Sustainable livelihoods framework

The sustainable livelihoods approach is a holistic and people centred approach to understanding and addressing the various and diverse factors that influence poverty or wellbeing and the typical relationships between these factors. This approach has been developed and adopted by a number of agencies, but most significant amongst them has been DFID, which produced a detailed framework and guidance materials (Figure 8). At the centre of this approach is an analysis of the resources or assets that poor people and communities have access to and use. These can include natural resources, skills, knowledge, health, access to education, sources of credit, or networks of social support. The extent of access to these assets is influenced by the prevailing social, institutional and political environment, which affects the ways in which people combine and use their assets to achieve their desired outcomes in life (for example increase income, wellbeing, food security etc)

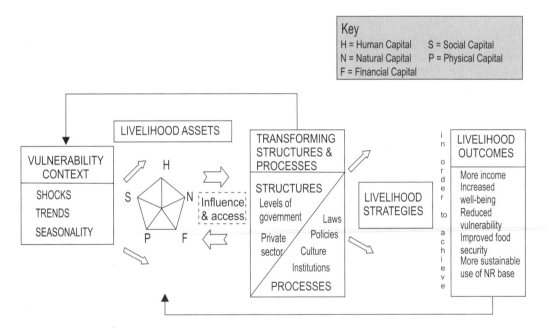

Figure 8. Sustainable livelihoods framework (DFID, 1999)

4.1.2 Pressure and release model

The pressure and release (PAR) model (Table 17) predicts that a disaster happens when a hazard meets a situation where vulnerability exists. A hazard occurring in the absence of a vulnerable situation will not cause a disaster. The basis for the PAR model is that a disaster is the interaction of two opposing forces; on the one side the processes generating vulnerability, and on the other, the hazard event. The model distinguishes between three levels of processes that contribute to vulnerability: unsafe conditions, dynamic pressures and root causes as illustrated below. These include social, economic, demographic and political, as well as physical factors. The model focuses on natural hazards, but is equally applicable to other types of hazards.

Table 17. Pressure and release model (Wisner *et al*, 1994)

Root causes	Dynamic stresses	Unsafe conditions	Disaster	Hazards
Limited access to • Power • Structure • Resources **Ideologies** • Political systems • Economic systems	**Lack of** • Local institutions • Training • Appropriate skills • Local investments • Markets • Press freedom • Ethical standards in public life **Macro-forces** • Rapid population change • Urbanization • Arms expenditure • Debt repayment • Deforestation • Decline in soil fertility	**Physical environment** • Dangerous locations • Unprotected buildings and infrastructure **Local economy** • Risky livelihoods • Low incomes **Social relations** • Groups at risk • Lack of local institutions **Public actions and institutions** • Lack of disaster preparedness • Prevalence of endemic diseases	**Risk = Hazard + Vulnerability**	• Earthquakes • Flooding • High winds • Cyclones • Hurricanes • Typhoons • Drought • Volcano eruptions • Landslides • Disease • Pests

4.1.3 Disaster Resilient Sustainable Livelihoods Framework

The Disaster Resilient Sustainable Livelihoods Framework (Figure 9) brings together disaster management issues with sustainable livelihoods, making links to the governance environment. It was developed from research and operational experience in South Asia led by Practical Action South Asia over a five-year period. Its main aim is to highlight the interrelationship between poverty, disaster risk and livelihoods at the conceptual and application levels, and to demand changes in policy, investment and practice from national governments in South Asia and international relief and development donors.

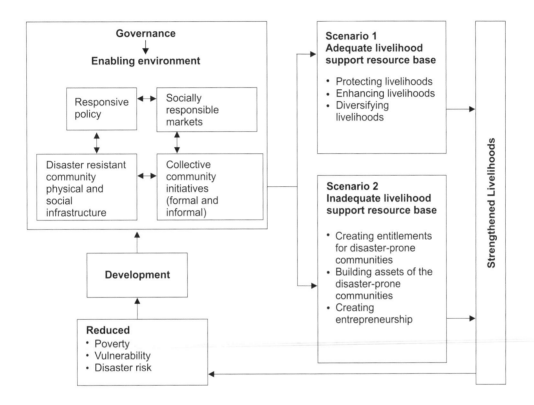

Figure 9. Disaster resilient sustainable livelihoods framework (Ariyabandu and Bhatti, 2005)

4.1.4 Practical Action's working model for achieving impact at scale

Practical Action's working model (Figure 10) is a framework for ensuring that projects and programmes achieve maximum impact by working at various levels to achieve change, including changing the policies and regulations of other organizations that have a wider reach than we do. The 'impact triangle' shows that as the scale of our impact increases up the model (width), our ability to measure or attribute it to our work (shade) decreases.

   Before beginning any activity, it is important to learn from past experience. New or improved ideas can be tested through projects. Rather than acting as a service delivery organization, we aim to add value and develop new learning which other, more appropriate organizations, can deliver at scale. This means working with local partners to build their capacity to replicate. Projects and programmes collect and analyse lessons so that we have convincing evidence showing how resilient livelihoods and communities can be achieved. This evidence can then be packaged and presented in ways that can be easily communicated to different target audiences to help them to make appropriate changes in practice. By getting larger agencies and donors to adopt and fund best practices, and ultimately internalize them through policy and regulatory change, we take a big step to achieving scale.

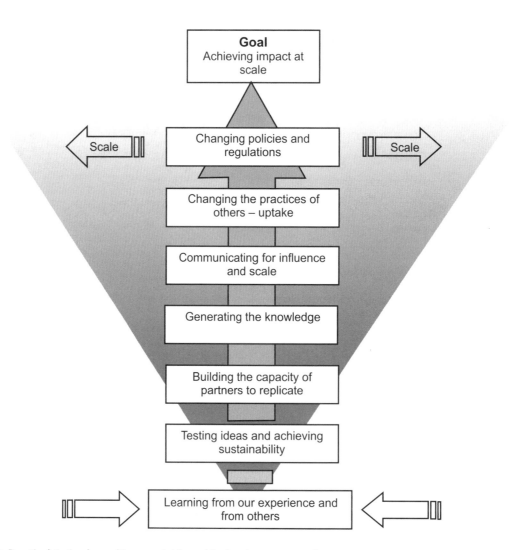

Figure 10. Practical Action's working model for achieving impact at scale

4.2 V2R ANALYSIS SUMMARY SHEETS

Sheet 1 Analysis of vulnerability outcomes

What to ask about vulnerability outcomes?

- What is the history of disasters in the community?
- Are there other events, circumstances or trends that they feel unable to cope with or adapt to?
- Are there households or social / livelihood groups which suffer periods of food insecurity.
- How do members of the community assess wealth (assets, education, inclusion, etc) and which social or livelihood groups are identified as poorest or unable to move out of poverty?

Suggested tools

- Secondary data: gather external data on disasters, livelihoods, food security, etc. in the area.
- Transect walk: make observations about the community, its resources and infrastructure, and general wellbeing of people.
- Timeline: understand broad history of disasters in the community or changes that they have had to adapt to.
- Key informant interviews: find out from community leaders about the different social and livelihood groups in the community, and their perceptions of their relative vulnerability.
- Wealth ranking: understand local indicators of poverty. Identify poorest and food insecure groups.

Collating the information

	Issues and vulnerabilities
History of disasters	
Other events or trends	
Groups suffering food insecurity	
Groups living in poverty	

Sheet 2 Analysis of hazards and stresses

What to ask about hazards and stresses?

- What is the typical frequency and duration of occurrence of this hazard or stress? Is it seasonal? Has it changed over time, for example due to climate change or other trends?
- What is the speed of onset of the hazard or stress? Are there any warning signs? Are there established early warning systems?
- Are there any underlying causes of the hazard or stress? Does the community understand them, or know how to address them?
- Which groups within the community (livelihood groups, social groups, geographical groups, people with disability, etc) are most affected and how?
- Which community or individual assets, property, or services are affected (for example infrastructure, services, markets, crops, savings, land) and how?
- How do different groups typically respond immediately after the hazard occurs (are there contingency plans, safe areas, emergency resources, response organizations, etc)?
- Based on the issues raised, what opportunities and capacities are available, or could be strengthened to improve peoples' disaster preparedness?

Suggested tools

- Secondary data: gather external data on hazards and vulnerable groups from relevant sources.
- Hazard map: identify geographical areas that are physically vulnerable for example to flood, landslide, etc.
- Hazard trend analysis: a development of the time line to better understand changes in hazard frequency, severity, or predictability over time. May be linked to climate change.
- Story telling: find out how people typically behave or respond after a hazard.
- Group discussion: discuss capacities and opportunities for improved disaster preparedness.

Collating the information

Hazard Priority 1 Drought	Issues and vulnerabilities	Capacities and opportunities for resilience
Frequency, Duration, Seasonality, Trends		
Warning signs, Early warning		
Underlying causes		
Groups affected		
Assets and services affected		
Immediate response		

Sheet 3 Livelihood analysis

What to ask about livelihoods?

- What are the principal livelihood groups within the community, and which of these groups are identified as socio-economically vulnerable or unable to cope and recover when a particular hazard or stress occurs?
- What kinds of coping strategies (positive or negative) do different people currently use when they are affected by hazards or stresses (particularly vulnerable livelihood groups).
- What are the key constraints and opportunities faced by each vulnerable livelihood group (for example organizational capacity, access to productive resources, access to skills and technologies, access to markets, secure living conditions)?
- Are their livelihoods affected by particular hazards, by climate change, or by other long term trends which should be explored further?
- What are the gaps and opportunities in relation to external institutions which affect their livelihoods (services, financial, safety nets?)

Suggested tools

- Secondary data: gather external data on principal livelihoods, resource constraints, markets, employment opportunities, service providers etc. in the area.
- Seasonal calendar: use to identify the livelihood activities throughout the year, and the different stresses or hazards that affect the resilience of those livelihoods.
- Ranking: focus group discussion with community leaders can identify principal livelihood groups in the community and which are identified as poor or vulnerable.
- Key informant or group interviews representing different vulnerable livelihood groups.

Collating the information

	Livelihood vulnerabilities and erosive coping strategies	Coping capacities and opportunities for resilience
Community organization		
Access to productive resources		
Skills and technologies		
Access to markets and employment		
Safe living conditions		

Sheet 4 Analysing future uncertainty

What to ask about long term trends including climate change?

- What significant trends or changes have people observed in recent decades?
- What are the impacts and implications of these on people's livelihoods and the incidence of hazards?
- How do people understand the causes of these trends or changes?
- Do people have access to relevant and timely information to help them adapt to those changes (for example future predictions, short term forecasting, adaptation strategies)?
- How are people adapting to change now? Do they have the necessary resources to be able to adapt (for example organizational capacity, access to productive resources, access to skills and technologies, access to markets, secure living conditions)?
- Do they feel confident about their ability to adapt to future changes?
- What institutional response has there been to the trends identified (awareness raising, mitigation, support, information and funding for adaptation)?
- What opportunities are there for influencing these trends, improving understanding, ensuring access to information and resources, and building confidence to adapt?

Suggested tools

- Secondary data: collect external data on climate, economic and other trends and impacts.
- Long term trend analysis: explore the historical patterns of issues that affect development, including social, economic, institutional and environmental issues over periods of between 10 and 40 years.
- Knowledge network mapping: explore different sources of information relating to climate change or other trends (for example medium term climate predictions, expected trends in crop or energy prices, technologies for climate adaptation, etc) using a venn diagram.
- Story telling and discussion: allow people to share experiences of how their livelihoods have been impacted by trends (such as climate change) and how they have attempted to cope or adapt. Discuss ways in which they could be better supported to adapt in the future.

Collating the information

Trend:	Issues and vulnerabilities	Capacities and opportunities for resilience
Observed changes and impacts		
Understanding		
Access to information		
Adaptation strategies		

Sheet 5 Governance analysis

What to ask about governance?

- Which organizations, policies, processes or underlying systemic issues are contributing to the occurrence of hazards, exposure to hazards, livelihood vulnerability, or future uncertainty? How or why are those organizations or policies contributing to vulnerability?
- Which organizations, policies or processes could help enable disaster preparedness, strengthen, livelihood security and diversification, or adaptive capacity?
- What opportunities exist for improving the governance environment: ensuring decentralized and participatory decision making, strengthening local to national links, promoting integrated approaches or addressing systemic issues?

Suggested tools for analysis

- Secondary data: collect external data on locally relevant organizations, policies, processes etc.
- Venn diagrams: use to map different livelihood and disaster preparedness service providers and their accessibility by the community as a starting point for discussion on institutional gaps and opportunities.
- Interviews: with key informants such as local government, NGO and private sector service providers to provide further insight into institutional limitations
- Market mapping: identify the different market chain actors and business environment factors and the various linkages between primary producers and final consumers to help identify bottlenecks and opportunities.

Collating your information

	Issues and vulnerabilities	Capacities and opportunities for resilience
Hazards and disaster preparedness		
Livelihoods		
Future uncertainty		

REFERENCES

Albu, M. (2010) *Emergency Market Mapping and Analysis Toolkit*, Practical Action Publishing, Rugby.

Ariyabandu, M.M. and A. Bhatti (2005) *Livelihood Centred Approach to Disaster Management. A Policy Framework for South Asia*. ITDG South Asia, Sri Lanka and Rural Development Policy Institute, Pakistan.

Benn, H. (2006) 'We Need an Emergency Service' *Developments Magazine*, May 2006, DFID http://www.developments.org.uk/articles/hilary-benn-we-need-an-emergency-service/

Cannon, T. (2008) *Reducing Peoples' Vulnerability to Natural Hazards. Communities and Resilience*. UNU-WIDER Research Paper 2008/34.

Chambers, R. (1989) Introduction In 'Vulnerability: How the Poor Cope', *IDS Bulletin*, vol. 20/2, IDS Brighton.

Coupe, S. and Pasteur, K. (2009) *Food and Livelihood Security Lesson Learning Study*. Practical Action UK, Internal Document.

DFID (1999) *Sustainable Livelihoods Guidance Sheets*, UK Department for International Development, London.

DFID (2005) *Disaster Risk Reduction*: A *Development Concern*, DFID Policy Briefing, http://www.dfid.gov.uk/Documents/publications/disaster-risk-reduction.pdf

Ensor, J. and Berger, R. (2009) *Governance for Community Based Adaptation*, Practical Action Discussion Paper, http://practicalaction.org/climate-change/docs/climate_change/governance-for-community-based-adaptation.pdf

Ensor, J. and Berger, R. (2009) *Understanding Climate Change Adaptation*, Practical Action Publishing, Rugby.

Global Network for Civil Society Organizations for Disaster Risk Reduction (2009) *'Clouds but Little Rain...'* Views from the Frontline, A local perspective of progress towards implementation of the Hyogo Framework for Action.

Green, D. (2008) *From Poverty to Power: How Active Citizens and Effective States Can Change the World*. Oxfam Publishing, Oxford http://www.oxfam.org/en/content/from-poverty-power-full-text

Griffith, A. and Osorio, L. E. (2008) *Participatory Market System Development: Best Practices in Implementation of Value Chain Development Programs*, USAID Best Practices in Implementation Series. http://www.microlinks.org/ev.php?ID=35558_201&ID2=DO_TOPIC

Gumbo, D. (2009) *Community Based Planning Guidelines*, Practical Action Southern Africa. http://practicalaction.org/docs/southern_africa/CBP_MANUAL_20May_2009.doc

IFRC (2002) *World Disaster Report 2002*, International Federation of the Red Cross and Red Crescent Societies, Switzerland.

ITDG South Asia and Rural Development Policy Institute (2005) *Livelihood Centred Approach to Disaster Management, A Policy Framework for South Asia*.

Pasteur, K. (ed) (2010) *Integrating Approaches: Sustainable Livelihoods, Disaster Risk Reduction and Climate Change Adaptation*, Practice Briefing, Practical Action, Rugby.

Practical Action South Asia (2010) *Decentralized Disaster Risk Management Training Manual*, Practical Action South Asia http://www.duryognivaran.org/ddrmt.php

Strengthening Climate Resilience Project http://www.eldis.org/go/topics/resource-guides/climate-change/key-issues/strenghtening-climate-resilience

Swift, J. (1989) 'Why are Rural People Vulnerable to Famine?' In 'Vulnerability: How the Poor Cope', *IDS Bulletin*, vol. 20/2, IDS Brighton.

Twigg, J. (2007) *Characteristics of a Disaster-resilient Community*, A Guidance Note, Version 1 for Field Testing. Benfield UCL Hazard Research Centre. www.benfieldhrc.org

UNDP (2007) *Human Development Report 2007*, United Nations Development Programme.

Venton, P. and S. La Trobe (2008) *Linking Climate Change Adaptation and Disaster Risk Reduction*, Tearfund, London.

Wisner, B., Blaikie, P., Cannon, T. and Davis, I. (1994) *At Risk, Natural Hazards, People's Vulnerability and Disasters*, Routledge, Oxford.

World Habitat Awards, *Post-tsunami Reconstruction and Rehabilitation in Sri Lanka*, Asoka Ajantha World Habitat Award finalist 2008 http://www.worldhabitatawards.org/winners-and-finalists/project-details.cfm?lang=00&theProjectID=986C2BBF-15C5-F4C0-99A7AA69AEC53694

RESOURCES

Vulnerability and resilience

Chambers, R. (1989) Introduction in 'Vulnerability: How the Poor Cope', *IDS Bulletin vol. 20/2*, Institute of Development Studies, Brighton.

Ariyabandu, M.M. and Bhatti, A. (2005) *Livelihood-centred Approach to Disaster Management,* A Policy Framework for South Asia, ITDG South Asia, Sri Lanka, and Rural Development Policy Institute, Pakistan.

UNISDR (2008) *Linking Disaster Risk Reduction and Poverty Reduction, Good Practices and Lessons Learned,* United Nations International Strategy for Disaster Reduction Secretariat, Geneva.
http://www.unisdr.org/eng/about_isdr/isdr-publications/14_Linking_Disaster_Risk_Reduction_Poverty_Reduction/Linking_Disaster_Risk_Reduction_Poverty_Reduction.pdf

UNISDR (2008) *Gender Perspectives: Integrating Disaster Risk Reduction Into Climate Change Adaptation, Good Practices And Lessons Learned,* United Nations International Strategy for Disaster Reduction Secretariat, Geneva.
http://www.unisdr.org/preventionweb/files/3391_GenderPerspectivesIntegratingDRRCCGood20Practices.pdf

Prevention and protection

Practical Action (2007) *Spurs and Dykes for Flood Water Protection,* Practical Action Technical Brief.
http://practicalaction.org/practicalanswers/product_info.php?cPath=57_89&products_id=222&attrib=1

UNEP (2007) *Environment and Vulnerability, Emerging Perspectives,* prepared on behalf of the UN ISDR Environment and Disaster Working Group, United Nations Environment Programme.
http://www.preventionweb.net/globalplatform/2007/first-session/docs/Workshops/4_2_3_Ecosystems_Environment/Environment_and_Vulnerability.pdf

Early warning and awareness

Practical Action (2009) *Early Warning Saving Lives, Nepal,* Practical Answers Video.
http://practicalaction.org/practicalanswers/product_info.php?cPath=57_89&products_id=415&attrib=2

Practical Action, *Early Warning Systems in Nepal* (web resource).
http://practicalaction.org/?id=dipecho&utm_campaign=Dipecho+EWS+Nepal

UNISDR (2006) *Developing Early Warning Systems, a Checklist,* Third International Conference on Early Warning, 27–29 March 2006, Bonn Germany.
http://www.unisdr.org/ppew/info-resources/ewc3/checklist/English.pdf

Understanding and Implementing Community-Based Early Warning Systems in the Context of Title II Programming, World Vision.
http://wvfoodresourcesworkshop.com/Images/mmDocument/CEWS%20Part%201-FINAL.pdf

UNISDR (2007) *Towards a Culture of Prevention: Disaster Risk Reduction Begins at School*, United Nations International Strategy for Disaster Reduction Secretariat, Geneva.
http://www.unisdr.org/eng/about_isdr/isdr-publications/11-education-good-practices/education-good-practices.pdf

Emergency planning

Practical Action Latin America (2007) *Emergency Preparedness Plans*, Practical Action Technical Brief.
http://practicalaction.org/practicalanswers/product_info.php?cPath=57_89&products_id=260&attrib=1

Practical Action (2007) *Are We Prepared? ¿Estamos preparados?, Learning From the Yungay Earthquake in 1970, Peru*, Practical Answers Video (Spanish with English subtitles).
http://practicalaction.org/practicalanswers/product_info.php?cPath=57_89&products_id=280&attrib=2

Build back better

Practical Action South Asia (2005) *Rebuilding Homes and Livelihoods,* Practical Action Technical Brief.
http://practicalaction.org/practicalanswers/product_info.php?cPath=57_90&products_id=216&attrib=1

Practical Action (no date) *Rebuilding in the Aftermath of an Earthquake,* Practical Action Technical Brief.
http://practicalaction.org/practicalanswers/product_info.php?cPath=57_90&products_id=256&attrib=1

Practical Action (no date) *Transitional Shelter - Essential Criteria to be Met,* Practical Action Technical Brief.
http://practicalaction.org/practicalanswers/product_info.php?cPath=57_90&products_id=267&attrib=1

Lyons, M., and Schilderman, T. (eds) (2010) *Building Back Better, Delivering People-Centred Housing Reconstruction at Scale,* Practical Action Publishing, Rugby.

Schilderman, T. and Lyons, M. (2010) *Putting People at the Centre of Reconstruction*. Practical Action Practice Briefing.
http://practicalaction.org/docs/access_to_services/PCR_Position_Paper.pdf

Livelihoods

DFID (1999) Sustainable Livelihoods Guidance Sheets, UK Department for International Development.
http://www.eldis.org/go/topics/dossiers/livelihoods-connect/what-are-livelihoods-approaches/training-and-learning-materials
Satge R. (2002) *Learning about Livelihoods: Insights from Southern Africa,* Oxfam, UK and Periperi, South Africa.
Pasteur, K. (2009) *Prioritising Marginalized Producers: Practical Action's Approach to Food and Livelihood Security,* Practical Action Programme Briefing.
http://practicalaction.org/reducing-vulnerability/docs/ia1/approach-to-food-and-livelihood-security.pdf

Strengthening community organization and voice

Blake, R. and Pasteur, K. (2010) *Empowering Community Organizations: A 'Light Touch' Approach for Long-term Impact,* Learning from Practice, Practical Action.
http://practicalaction.org/reducing-vulnerability/docs/ia1/empowering-community-organizations.pdf
Crowley, E., Baas, S., Termine, P., Rouse, J., Pozarny, P., and Dionne, G. (2005) *Organizations of the Poor: Conditions for Success.* United Nations Food and Agriculture Organization.
http://www.fao.org/sd/dim_in3/docs/in3_050901a1_en.pdf

Access to, and sustainable management of, natural resources

Cotula, L., Toulmin, C. and Quan, J. (2006) *Better Land Access for the Rural Poor: Lessons From Experience and Challenges Ahead,* IIED Land Tenure and Resources in Africa Series, International Institute for Environment and Development, London.
http://www.iied.org/pubs/pdfs/12532IIED.pdf
German, L., Kidane, B. and Mekonnen, K. (2005) *Watershed Management to Counter Farming Systems Decline: Toward a Demand-driven, Systems-oriented Research Agenda,* Agricultural Research and Extension Network Paper 145. Overseas Development Institute, London.
http://www.odi.org.uk/resources/download/4252.pdf
Lewins, R., Coupe, S. and Murray, F. (2008) *Voices from the Margins: Consensus Building with the Poor in Bangladesh,* Practical Action Publishing, Rugby.
Practical Action (2010) *Consensus Building with Participatory Action Plan Development,* Facilitator's Guide, Practical Action Publishing, Rugby.

Access to technologies

Ensor, J. (2010) *Technology for Adapting to Climate Change,* Practical Action Briefing
http://practicalaction.org/climate-change/docs/climate_change/technology-for-adapting-to-climate-change.pdf
Murwira, K., Wedgewood, H., Watson, C. and Win, E. (2000) *Beating Hunger: The Chivi Experience: A Community-Based Approach to Food Security in Zimbabwe.* Practical Action Publishing.

Technologies for disaster resilient agriculture

Practical Action (2005) *Community Cereal Bank,* Practical Action Technical Brief.
http://practicalaction.org/practicalanswers/product_info.php?cPath=57_89&products_id=50&attrib=1
Practical Action (2006) *Floating Gardens in Bangladesh,* Practical Action Technical Brief.
http://practicalaction.org/practicalanswers/product_info.php?cPath=24_79&products_id=201&attrib=1
Practical Action (no date) *Seed Fairs,* Practical Action Technical Brief.
http://practicalaction.org/practicalanswers/product_info.php?cPath=24_80&products_id=61&attrib=1
Practical Action (2006) *Integrated Soil Fertility,* Practical Action Technical Brief.
http://practicalaction.org/practicalanswers/product_info.php?cPath=24_77&products_id=55&attrib=1
Practical Action (2007) *Micro Irrigation,* Practical Action Technical Brief.
http://practicalaction.org/practicalanswers/product_info.php?cPath=24_78&products_id=56&attrib=1

Access to markets and employment

Albu, M. and Griffith, A. (2005) *Mapping the Market,* Practical Action Mimeo, June 2005.
http://practicalaction.org/docs/ia2/mapping_the_market.pdf
Albu, M. and Griffith, A. (2006) 'Mapping the Market: Participatory Market Chain Development in Practice', *Small Enterprise Development* vol.17/2.
http://practicalaction.org/docs/ia2/mapping_the_market_albu_griffith_sedj-june2006.pdf
Albu, M. (2010) *Emergency Market Mapping and Analysis Toolkit,* Practical Action Publishing, Rugby.

Ensuring safe living conditions

Practical Action (2008) *Earthquake-Resistant Housing*, Practical Action Technical Brief.
  http://practicalaction.org/practicalanswers/product_info.php?cPath=57&products_id=135&attrib=1
Practical Action (2009) *Ensuring Safe Drinking Water in Bangladesh*, Practical Action
  http://www.practicalaction.org/reducing-vulnerability/docs/ia1/safe-drinking-water-bangladesh.pdf
Practical Action (2010) *Flood Resistant Housing: Adapting to Climate Change in Bangladesh*, accessed 2nd September 2010.
  http://practicalaction.org/disaster-reduction/flood-resistant_housing

Future uncertainty

Berger, R. and Ensor, J. (2009) *Understanding Adaptation to Climate Change: Lessons from Community-based Approaches*, Practical Action Publishing.
Ensor, J. (2009) *Bio-Diverse Agriculture for a Changing Climate*, Practical Action Briefing Paper.
  http://www.practicalaction.org/advocacy/docs/advocacy/biodiverse-agriculture-for-a-changing-climate.pdf
Clements, R., Cossío, M. and Ensor, J. (eds) (2010) Climate Change Adaptation in Peru: The Local Experiences.
  http://www.solucionespracticas.org.pe/publicacionessp/publicacion_ok.php?id=NTAw

Governance

Ensor, J. and Berger, R. (2009) *Governance for Community Based Adaptation*, Practical Action Discussion Paper.
  http://practicalaction.org/climate-change/docs/climate_change/governance-for-community-based-adaptation.pdf
Lewins, R., and Coupe, S. (2001) *Negotiating the Seed Treaty*, Practical Action Publishing, Rugby
Pasteur, K. (ed) (2010) *Integrating Approaches: Sustainable Livelihoods, Disaster Risk Reduction and Climate Change Adaptation.*
  http://practicalaction.org/reducing-vulnerability/docs/ia1/integrating-approaches-esrc-briefing-paper.pdf
Taha, A., Lewins, R., Coupe, S. and Peacocke, B. (2010) *Consensus building with Participatory Action Plan Development*, Practical Action, Rugby.
  http://practicalaction.org/reducing-vulnerability/participatory-action-plan-development
UNISDR (2005) *Governance: Institutional and Policy Frameworks for Risk Reduction*, Thematic Discussion Paper Cluster 1, World Conference on Disaster Reduction, January 2005, Kobe, Japan.
  http://www.unisdr.org/wcdr/thematic-sessions/WCDR-discussion-paper-cluster1.pdf
UNISDR (2010) *Local Government and Disaster Risk Reduction*, Good Practices and Lessons Learned, UNISDR, Geneva.
  http://www.unisdr.org/eng/risk-reduction/local-governments/UNISDR-Flyer-Local-Goverments.pdf
Windfur, M and Jonsen, J. (2005) *Food Sovereignty. Towards Democracy in Localized Food Systems*, Practical Action Publishing, Rugby.

Vulnerability and capacity analysis

ActionAid (no date) *Participatory Vulnerability Analysis, A Step-by-step Guide for Field Staff*, ActionAid, London.
  http://www.actionaid.org.uk/doc_lib/108_1_participatory_vulnerability_analysis_guide.pdf
Albu, M. (2010) *Emergency Market Mapping and Analysis Toolkit*. Practical Action Publishing, Rugby.
FAO (2001) *Socio-Economic and Gender Analysis* (SEAGA). Field Handbook. Food and Agriculture Organization, Rome.
  http://www.gdnonline.org/resources/seaga-field-handbook.pdf
IFAD (2009) *Guidance Notes for Institutional Analysis in Rural Development Programmes*, International Fund for Agricultural Development, Rome.
  http://www.ifad.org/english/institutions/
LEGS (2009) *Livestock Emergency Guidelines and Standards (LEGS)*, Practical Action Publishing, Rugby.
  http://www.livestock-emergency.net/downloads/index.html
Practical Action (no date) *Preparation of Risk Maps*, Practical Action Technical Briefs.
  http://practicalaction.org/practicalanswers/product_info.php?cPath=57_89&products_id=215&attrib=1
Venton, P. and Hansford, B. (2006) *Reducing Risk of Disaster in our Communities*, Roots 9, Tearfund, London.
  http://tilz.tearfund.org/Publications/ROOTS/Reducing+risk+of+disaster+in+our+communities.htm
Wiggins, S. (2009) *Climate Change and Environmental Degradation Risk and Adaptation Assessment (CEDRA)*, Tearfund, Teddington.
  http://tilz.tearfund.org/Topics/Environmental+Sustainability/CEDRA.htm

Community and project planning

Gumbo, D. (2009) *Community Based Planning Guidelines*, Practical Action Southern Africa.
  http://practicalaction.org/docs/southern_africa/CBP_MANUAL_20May_2009.doc
Ullah, B., Shahnaz. F. and Van Den Ende, P. (eds) (2009) *Good Practices for Community Resilience*, Practical Action Bangladesh, Dhaka.
  http://practicalaction.org/disaster-livelihoods/docs/ia1/good-practices-community-resiliance-052009.pdf

Monitoring and evaluation

Twigg, J. (2007) *Characteristics of a Disaster Resilient Community*, A Guidance Note, Aon Benfield UCL Hazard Research Centre.
     http://www.proventionconsortium.org/?pageid=90
Wageningen International (no date), *Participatory Planning, Monitoring and Evaluation. Managing for Learning and Impact in Rural Development.*
     http://portals.wi.wur.nl/ppme/

Capacity building

Practical Action South Asia (2010) *Decentralized Disaster Risk Management Training Manual*, Practical Action South Asia.
     http://www.duryognivaran.org/ddrmt.php
Practical Action Zimbabwe (forthcoming) 'Livelihood-centred disaster risk reduction – a manual for Zimbabwe', Practical Action Zimbabwe.
     http://practicalaction.org/reducing-vulnerability/publications

GLOSSARY

Acceptable risk

The level of potential losses that a society or community considers acceptable given existing social, economic, political, cultural, technical and environmental conditions.

Adaptive capacity

The combination of assets, skills, technologies and confidence to make changes and adapt effectively to the challenges posed by long term trends, such as climate change.

Capacity

The combination of all the strengths, attributes and resources available within a community, society or organization that can be used to achieve agreed goals.

Capacity Building

The process by which people, organizations and society systematically stimulate and develop their capacities over time to achieve social and economic goals, including by improving knowledge, skills, systems and institutions.

Climate change

A change in the climate that persists for decades or longer, arising from either natural causes or human activity.

Climate Change Adaptation

The adjustment in natural or human systems in response to actual or expected climatic stimuli or their effects, which moderates harm or exploits beneficial opportunities. Adaptation includes changes in management activities, institutional settings and infrastructure that enables effective response to the changes in climate that may occur.

Contingency planning

A management process that analyses specific potential events or emerging situations that might threaten society or the environment and establishes arrangements in advance to enable timely, effective and appropriate responses to such events and situations.

Coping strategies

The strategies that households and communities use, based on available skills and resources, to face, manage and recover from adverse conditions, emergencies or disasters in the short term.

Disaster

A serious disruption of the functioning of a community or a society involving widespread human, material, economic or environmental losses and impacts, which exceeds the ability of the affected community or society to cope using its own resources.

Disaster risk

The potential disaster losses, in lives, health status, livelihoods, assets and services, which could occur to a particular community or a society over some specified future time period. Risk refers to the probability of a negative outcome (such as a disaster). When we talk about risk we are recognizing the element of uncertainty. The degree of risk or probability depends on the probability of the hazard occurring combined with the degree of livelihood insecurity.

Disaster risk reduction

The concept and practice of reducing disaster risks through systematic efforts to analyse and manage the causal factors of disasters, including reduced exposure to hazards, improved preparedness for adverse events, strengthening of livelihoods, wise management of land and the environment, and an appropriate institutional and policy environment.

Early warning system

The set of capacities needed to generate and disseminate timely and meaningful warning information to enable individuals, communities and organizations threatened by a hazard to prepare and to act appropriately and in sufficient time to reduce the possibility of harm or loss.

Ecosystem services

The benefits people derive from ecosystems, including provisioning services such as food and water; regulating services such as flood and disease control; cultural services such as spiritual, recreational, and cultural benefits; and supporting services such as nutrient cycling that maintain the conditions for life on Earth.

Environmental degradation

The reduction of the capacity of the environment to meet social and ecological objectives and needs.

Exposure

People, property, systems, or other elements present in hazard zones that are thereby subject to potential losses.

Governance environment

The range of different formal and informal organizations, policies and practices operating at different levels from local to international.

Hazard

A dangerous phenomenon, substance, human activity or condition that may cause loss of life, injury or other health impacts, property damage, loss of livelihoods and services, social and economic disruption, or environmental damage.

Livelihoods

The resources (including skills, technologies, organizations) and activities required to make a living and have a good quality of life. A livelihood is therefore not just what someone does for a living, i.e. a job, but includes the different skills and resources that they draw on both to sustain their physical and economic needs, but also to fulfil their spiritual and social needs.

Long term trends

Patterns of change over time such as population change, resource use or degradation, technology development, and social change. They can be either positive or negative. Climate change is an important long term trend.

Mitigation

The lessening or limitation of the adverse impacts of hazards and related disasters.

Preparedness

The knowledge and capacities developed by governments, professional response and recovery organizations, communities and individuals to effectively anticipate, respond to, and recover from, the impacts of likely, imminent or current hazard events or conditions.

Prevention

The avoidance of the adverse impacts of hazards and related disasters.

Recovery

The restoration, and improvement where appropriate, of facilities, livelihoods and living conditions of disaster-affected communities, including efforts to reduce disaster risk factors.

Resilience

The ability of a system, community or society to resist, absorb, cope with and recover from the effects of hazards and to adapt to longer term changes in a timely and efficient manner without enduring detriment to food security or wellbeing.

Response

The provision of emergency services and public assistance during or immediately after a disaster in order to save lives, reduce health impacts, ensure public safety and meet the basic subsistence needs of the people affected.

Risk

The combination of the probability of an event and its negative consequences.

Risk assessment

A methodology to determine the nature and extent of risk by analysing potential hazards and evaluating existing conditions of vulnerability that together could potentially harm exposed people, property, services, livelihoods and the environment on which they depend.

Risk management

The systematic approach and practice of managing uncertainty to minimize potential harm and loss.

Stresses

Smaller, low impact events, and seasonal factors (for example employment, prices, health) can undermine livelihoods.

Sustainable development

Development that meets the needs of the present without compromising the ability of future generations to meet their own needs.

Vulnerability

The degree to which a population or system is susceptible to, and unable to cope with hazards and stresses, including the effects of climate change.

The glossary draws heavily on: UNISDR (2009) *Terminology on Disaster Risk Reduction*, United Nations International Strategy for Disaster Reduction Secretariat.
http://www.unisdr.org/preventionweb/files/7817_UNISDRTerminologyEnglish.pdf